1. Killing Me Softly

KILLING ME SOFTLY

Books by the Same Author

The Starved And The Silent
Poverty: Sign of Our Times
To Live Is Christ: The Sisters of Mary Book of Spirituality

KILLING ME SOFTLY

The Inspiring Story of a Champion of the Poor

Msgr. Aloysius Schwartz

ALBA·HOUSE   NEW·YORK

SOCIETY OF ST. PAUL, 2187 VICTORY BLVD., STATEN ISLAND, NEW YORK 10314

Library of Congress Cataloging-in-Publication Data

Schwartz, Aloysius.
  Killing me softly: the inspiring story of a champion of the poor
/ Aloysius Schwartz.
        p. cm.
    ISBN 0-8189-0685-5
    1. Schwartz, Aloysius. 2. Catholic Church — Clergy — Biography.
  3. Church work with the poor. 4. Amyotrophic lateral sclerosis —
  Patients — Biography. I. Title.
  BX4705.S51437A3   1993
  282'.092 — dc20   93-32689
  [B]   CIP

Nihil Obstat:
Msgr. Benedicto S. Aquino
Vice Chancellor

Imprimatur:
† Jaime L. Cardinal Sin
Archbishop of Manila
October 7, 1992

The Nihil Obstat and Imprimatur are official declarations
that a book or pamphlet is free of doctrinal or moral
error. No implication is contained therein that those
who have granted the Nihil Obstat and Imprimatur agree
with the contents, opinions or statements expressed.

Printed in the United States of America by the
Fathers and Brothers of the Society of St. Paul,
2187 Victory Boulevard, Staten Island, New York 10314,
as part of their communications apostolate.

ISBN: 0-8189-0685-5

Printing Information:

Current Printing - first digit 1 2 3 4 5 6 7 8 9 10

Year of Current Printing - first year shown

| 1993 | 1994 | 1995 | 1996 | 1997 | 1998 |

Dedicated to

MARY
Our Lady of Banneux
Virgin of the Poor

Acknowledgments

I would like to thank Monsignor Schwartz' sister, Dolores Vita, for the many hours she spent working on *Killing Me Softly*.

Due to the debilitating effects of his affliction with Amyotrophic Lateral Sclerosis, Monsignor Schwartz had to dictate this book. He died one week after completing the cassette tape for the last chapter. Following his death, Dolores finished typing the book, organized the chapters and did other related jobs needed to complete this book.

I would like also to thank Tom and Glory Sullivan for providing the services of Charlene Ikonomou and other members of their staff at Government Institutes, Inc., who assisted with copy editing, proofing and preparing the book for printing. Tom also contacted Alba House on behalf of the Sisters of Mary and helped secure and finalize an agreement to have this book published.

Lastly, I would like to thank the people who have continuously supported Monsignor Schwartz in his works. It is through these generous friends and through the blessings of God that Monsignor Schwartz prospered in his service to the poor.

Sister Michaela
Superior General
The Sisters of Mary

Table of Contents

Foreword

The task of spreading the gospel to all creatures as entrusted by our Lord to His Apostles found fulfillment in an oustanding manner in the life and death of Monsignor Aloysius Schwartz. Such is the essential content of this book, *Killing Me Softly* which Monsignor Schwartz wrote himself. From his native land in the first world he embarked to work in the second world and eventually arrived in this third world country of the Philippines simply to serve the poor children and the sick people whom our Lord desired to be blessed in care and love.

Monsignor Schwartz' adherence to Christ as wonderfully narrated in this book serves as a fitting homage to the heavenly grace which has sustained him to consummate the self-offering to the gospel he began since the moment he realized his vocation.

May the life of Monsignor Schwartz serve as an encouragement to our dedicated apostles who desire a true to life account of someone totally devoted to the service of the Lord's beloved, the poor children and the sick people in whom we can encounter and serve God so as to inherit the blessings of the kingdom.

† *JAIME L. CARDINAL SIN*
Archbishop of Manila
June, 1993

Introduction

Killing Me Softly was written by Father Aloysius Schwartz who was recently nominated a second time for the Nobel Peace Prize. Father Al was a missionary priest for over 35 years who founded charity programs in Korea, the Philippines, and Mexico.

Among the charity programs he established during his 35 years of service to the poor are Boystowns and Girlstowns in three countries that now care for a total of more than 15,000 underprivileged children. These children range in age from day one through high school. They receive a fully accredited high school education and also learn valuable vocational skills. The girls learn dressmaking, industrial sewing machine operation, steno-typing and book-keeping, electronics, and basic computer systems while the boys learn machine shop, auto mechanics and driving, refrigeration and air conditioning. These skills enable graduates of Father Al's Boystowns and Girlstowns to find good jobs and insures that they no longer face a life of struggle and poverty.

In addition, he erected two full service hospitals for the poor in Korea, which serve over 600 patients and established the largest tuberculosis sanitarium in the Philippines which provides free medical care to over 2,300 destitute patients. He also started the Village of Life, a home for destitute, homeless, and handicapped men in Korea. The Village of Life provides vocational training for able bodied residents. As a result of this training, some of the men are able to work part-time at such jobs as bag making and helping to care for the retarded children. Working helps the men develop a sense of self-worth. They use their earnings to help support themselves.

In 1964, Father Al founded an order of nuns called the Sisters of Mary, who now number over 200. Our Lady of Banneux, "The Virgin of the Poor," is the patroness of the Sisters of Mary. This smiling virgin of the poor, who came to relieve suffering, is the living book from whom the Sisters of Mary learn the nature of their calling. The motto of the Sisters of Mary is, "Let Us Serve the Lord with Joy!" The Sisters of Mary operate the many charity programs established by Father Schwartz. These programs now serve more than 19,000 needy children and adults.

In 1981, Father founded the Brothers of Christ, which now has 12 members. The Brothers of Christ care for the 2,000 homeless men at the Village of Life.

In October of 1989, Father was diagnosed with amyotrophic lateral sclerosis (ALS) which is commonly known as "Lou Gehrig's" disease. In "Killing Me Softly," Father Al details the last couple of years of his life. The book has four major themes.

First, it details the life of a patient afflicted with ALS. The reader gains insight into the tremendous challenges a patient with ALS must face to survive from day to day with this terminal illness.

Second, the book details key events in Father Schwartz' life as a missionary priest. The events chronicled occurred primarily during the last couple of years of Father's life while he was battling ALS. Nonetheless, these events provide an insight into his unique and highly successful approach to helping the many underprivileged children and adults served by his charity programs. During this time period, Father had some remarkable achievements. As just one example, he expanded his Boystowns and Girlstowns program to a third country, Mexico. Expansion into Mexico involved travel from Korea and the Philippines, the purchase of land, construction of Boystowns and Girlstowns facilities, and recruitment of candidates. Despite his serious illness, Father with the help of the Sisters of Mary, was able to complete the first phase of what he called his "unfinished symphony" in a period of less than two years. Prior to his death he dedicated the initial buildings in Mexico and welcomed the first children.

Third, Father Al describes friends and saints who had a tremendous influence on his work. These include Sister Saint Gertrude, a Carmelite, Sister Vincent, one of Father's own Sisters of Mary, Saint Therese of Lisieux, and Mary, Our Lady of Banneux, the Virgin of the Poor. In discussing the lessons he learned from these saints, Father shares with the reader his own unique philosophy of service to the poor.

Fourth the book is Father Al's last will and testament to the Sisters of Mary. Father outlines his plans for the continued growth of the charity programs he established. He also names Sister Michaela as his successor. Sister Michaela worked with Father Al for almost 30 years and is one of the original Sisters of Mary. The many programs established by Father continue today under the direction of Sister Michaela and the Sisters of Mary.

This introduction would not be complete without a few words about how Father Al wrote "Killing Me Softly." Because he was unable to move his limbs due to the effects of ALS, he could not write or type this book. Father dictated a draft into a cassette recorder with the help of several of the Sisters of Mary. He shipped the cassette tapes from the Philippines to the United States where they were later typed onto a computer. At the time the tapes were shipped they represented the only copy of the book. If it were not for reliable overseas mail service, this book would have never been completed.

Due to his debilitating condition, Father was not able to review or edit the typed draft. In fact, he dictated the last chapter of the book one week prior to his death on March 16, 1992. He dictated guidelines for editing the book. He asked that we review grammar, edit out repetition, and that we keep the sentences and paragraphs short. We did our best to comply with his request and any editing of his original draft was minimal. We think you will agree that the resulting quality of Father's writing is remarkable given the constraints he faced with his illness.

Finally, Father's personal motto was a quotation by St. Irenaeus, **"The glory of God is man fully alive."** He loved it because it described his work with the poor in Korea, the Philippines, and Mexico. Father knew that every time a needy child or adult was raised up from the slums and given medical attention, food, clean clothing, a safe place to live, and an education, that

God's work was being done. With that in mind, he helped needy children and adults every day of his life to come alive to their full potential in this world.

Despite his illness and his physical limitations, Father remained fully alive in his service to God's poor until his death. We hope that his book *Killing Me Softly* will inspire the reader to utilize his or her talents to their fullest potential to give glory to God. We also hope that the book will serve as a remembrance of Father Al and encourage his friends to continue to support the many fine charity programs he established.

Joseph Vita, Nephew
August 15, 1993

Timeline

September 18, 1930 Born in Washington, D.C.

1936—1944 Holy Name Elementary School; Washington, D.C.

1944—1948 St. Charles Minor Seminary; Catonsville, Maryland

1948—1952 Maryknoll College, B.A. Degree; Glen Ellen, Illinois

1953—1957 Theology, Louvain University; Louvain, Belgium

June 29, 1957 Ordination to the priesthood; St. Martin's Church, Washington, D.C.; Bishop McNamara, Auxiliary Bishop of Washington

December 8, 1957 Arrived in Korea. Incardinated in the Diocese of Pusan, Korea

January 20, 1958 Afflicted with hepatitis; returned to U.S. for recuperation

1959 - 1961 Toured U.S. and Europe with Korean Bishop to raise money for the missions

March 1961 Established Korean Relief, Inc. (now called Asian Relief, Inc.) fund raising operation; Washington, D.C.

December 1961 Returned to Korea

June 1962 Appointed Pastor of Song-do Parish; Pusan, Korea

Summer 1963 Initiated Operation Hanky Self-help Embroidery Program, employing 3,000 slum dwellers; program continued until 1969

KILLING ME SOFTLY

August 15, 1964	Started family-unit orphan program, accepted first group of children
August 15, 1964	Founded the Sisters of Mary (Religious Group now numbering over 200 working in Korea, Philippines & Mexico); Pusan, Korea
Spring 1966	Published *The Starved and the Silent*, Doubleday
September 1, 1966	Opened the first dispensary in slums; Amidong, Pusan, Korea
January 18, 1967	Opened two more slum dispensaries; Amnamdong and Bosudong, Pusan, Korea
October 31, 1967	Resigned as pastor to work full time with Orphan Program
Spring 1968	Published *Poverty: Sign of Our Times*, Alba House
December 10, 1968	Built Amidong Middle School Free School for slum children; Pusan, Korea
July 1, 1969	Took over operation of Beggar's Hospice, serving 100 sick and dying vagrants; Pusan, Korea
October 30, 1969	Completed Amnamdong building, intended to be middle school for boys; became first Boystown; Pusan, Korea
April 10, 1970	Received 300 vagrant boys; started Boystown program in earnest
October 25, 1970	Built Sisters of Mary Hospital, 120 bed full-service hospital for the poor; Pusan, Korea
December 1972	Built second Boystown in Pusan, Korea
March 1, 1973	Opened Pusan Boystown elementary school
March 1, 1974	Opened Pusan Boystown Middle School
January 1, 1975	Started Boystown Program; Seoul, Korea
May 28, 1975	Received the Korean Presidential Medal Order of Civil Merit
March 1, 1976	Opened Technical High School; Pusan, Korea
May 16, 1976	Received the Korean National Award; first time awarded to a foreigner
May 29, 1977	Received honorary doctorate: "Doctor of Humane Letters"; Fordham University
August 15, 1977	Inaugurated second Boystown; Seoul, Korea

Timeline

July 1978	Began Girlstown Program; Pusan, Korea (The Boystown/Girlstown Programs now serving 4,000 orphans in Pusan and Seoul, Korea)
January 6, 1981	Began program for 400 severely retarded children; Seoul, Korea
January 6, 1981	Took over camp for 1,800 destitute and homeless men from City of Seoul, Korea
May 10, 1981	Founded the Society of Christ Religious Order of Men who care for the homeless men in Seoul
November 1, 1981	Dedicated Boystown Middle School; Pusan, Korea
February 11, 1982	Named Honorary Citizen; Pusan, Korea
June 29, 1982	Built Sisters of Mary Hospital 120 bed full-service hospital for the poor; Seoul, Korea
June 29, 1982	25th Anniversary of Ordination to Priesthood
August 30, 1983	Received Magsaysay Award for International Understanding Given by Rockefeller Brothers Foundation; Manila, Philippines
May 29, 1984	Dedicated Village of Life building now serving 2,000 homeless men; Seoul, Korea
1984	Nominated for the Nobel Peace Prize by Congressman Steny Hoyer (D-Maryland)
February 12, 1985	Arrived in Manila at invitation of Cardinal Sin to begin Boystown/Girlstown Program; Manila, Philippines
July 15, 1985	Began Medical Program for destitute tuberculosis patients Quezon Institute; Manila, Philippines
August 15, 1986	Inaugurated Boystown/Girlstown, now serving over 3,500 youngsters; Manila, Philippines
August 25, 1988	Received the Mother Teresa Award, Chamber of Commerce; Manila, Philippines
June 1989	Inaugurated the Sisters of Mary Charity Pavilions; Quezon Institute; complete renovation of facility; now serving 2,000 TB patients; Manila, Philippines

August 29, 1989	Inaugurated Girlstown & Gymnasium; now serving 800 girls; Pusan, Korea
October, 1989	Afflicted with Amyotrophic Lateral Sclerosis (Lou Gehrig's disease)
February 1, 1990	Elevated to Right Reverend Monsignor, Investiture Ceremony; Manila, Philippines
June 14, 1990	Inaugurated indoor swimming pool; Pusan, Korea
August 23, 1990	Inaugurated Boystown/Girlstown Program; now serving 3,000 youngsters; Talisay, Cebu, Philippines
September 12, 1990	Purchased property, Villa de los Ninos, to begin Boystown/Girlstown Program; Chalco, Mexico
October 1, 1990	Celebrated 60th birthday in Korea; 1,000 graduates returned for party
January 6, 1991	Blessing of new swimming pool in Talisay, Cebu, Philippines
July 23, 1991	Inaugurated Boystown Program; now serving 3,200 boys; Silang, Cavite, Philippines
September 1991	Published *To Live Is Christ: The Sisters of Mary Book of Spirituality*, Government Institutes
October 7, 1991	Inaugurated Boystown/Girlstown Program; now serving 2,100 youngsters; Chalco, Mexico
November 1, 1991	Ordination of Father Joseph Kim, seminarian; sponsored by Father Al; now serving the children in Pusan & Seoul
December 5, 1991	Special Recipient 1991 National Caring Award
February 6, 1992	Second nomination for the Nobel Peace Prize by U.S. Congressman Robert K. Dornan (R-California) *and* William D. Schaefer, Governor of Maryland
March 7, 1992	Completed his fourth book, *Killing Me Softly*
March 16, 1992	Father Aloysius Schwartz died in Manila, Philippines

Chapter 1

Crossing the River

G eronimo, the famous Indian chief, is reported to have said: "The way to cross a river is to cross it." In line with this wisdom, the way to write a book is to write it. This book has been in the back of my mind for a long time now, but for one reason or another, I have put off beginning it. This morning, however, I decided simply to plunge into the river and see where it takes me. Although my mind is a bit muddled concerning the form, the content and the purpose of the book, and although I have many misgivings, I have decided simply to begin writing it.

The title of the book, "Killing Me Softly," is taken from a song, the title of which escapes me. Perhaps this is the title, I don't know. I asked the sisters not long ago if any of them knew the title, and although none did, one sister told me confidently that she did know the name of the artist who sang it. His name was William Andrews she said. After a somewhat lengthy exchange, we decided that William Andrews was none other than Andy Williams. (Later I discovered it was Perry Como who recorded the song in 1973 and it was titled, "Killing Me Softly with Her Song.") So, we have the singer and the song. It matters little. These words, however, aptly describe the disease with which I am now afflicted. It is called amyotrophic lateral sclerosis (ALS) — more popularly, "Lou Gehrig's disease." It is a terminal illness which kills but ever so slowly, ever so cruelly, ever so softly.

In this opening chapter, it may be of interest to the reader to describe the mechanics by which this book is being composed. My hands and arms are now almost totally paralyzed. I no longer have the luxury of being able to put my thoughts on paper by pencil, pen or typewriter. I am not a very natural, gifted, spontaneous writer. My best work comes from much writing, rewriting and re-rewriting. After much effort and work, I can occasionally come up with a piece of writing with which I am more or less satisfied.

Now I must first compose in my mind what I want to put on paper. Then I record on a cassette tape. Someone transcribes my recorded words and, hopefully, the finished product will be a book. This process sounds simple enough but my experience proves nothing in life is really simple. Something as easy as making a cassette tape usually turns into something of a challenge and an adventure for me.

Here at our Boystown and Girlstown in the Philippines where I am currently working on this book, there must be close to a hundred tape recorders of various models, sizes, shapes and colors. At any given time, however, only a small percentage of these machines function properly and perfectly. Why this should be is another matter but the fact is undeniable. This would be okay except one never really knows which of the recorders are functioning at any given point in time. So it is that even recording becomes a high-risk venture. I have had the frustrating experience of recording my innermost thoughts and pouring out the secrets of my soul for one hour only to play it back and discover that I produced a blank tape.

This morning, I requested that Sister bring me a tape recorder that was working properly. The first one she brought me did not work nor did the second. The machine I am now using is the third which she put before me. The first microphone did not function either and the mike I am currently talking into is the second which was prepared for me.

I usually begin every recording session by talking to the machine with which I am working in order to make it "user friendly." In this, I am following the example of St. Francis of Assisi who spoke to the birds, and St. Anthony of Padua who is supposed to have preached to the fish.

The machine I am now looking at and working with is a big, heavy, black monster of some exotic Japanese make. However, I try to make a friend of it by shameless charm, cajolery and flattery. "Others may say," I begin, "that you are big and black, heavy and ugly, but I think you are very attractive and beautiful. What's more, I want very much that we be friends and work happily together. All I ask of you, dear friend and beautiful recorder, is that you do your duty according to your state of life — which of course is to take down my words as I speak them and to play them back obediently when called upon." I think I have captured the heart of this big monster by this sweet talk and that it will cooperate with me. It is obvious, if you are reading these pages, that this machine, or at least some machine, has consented to comply and cooperate.

To get back to ALS with which I am currently afflicted, it usually kills its victims by slow paralysis within a period of three years. In some patients, the time frame is shorter and in others, it is longer. But the average length of time from diagnosis to death is three years. I am now well into my third and most likely final year. Already, the disease has begun to attack my swallowing, speaking and breathing muscles. My voice is quite weak and sounds low, strained and husky. My pronunciation seems somewhat slurred. It is very possible, or better yet, very probable, that within six weeks or so, my voice will no longer be a viable instrument of communication for me. So, if I want to complete this book, I better get on with it and do so before my voice fails me.

I am writing this book for many people, but mostly for the Sisters of Mary, my daughters in Christ. The sisters are not only my daughters but also my friends in Christ. In Him, I feel that our hearts are one.

One of the characteristics of true friendship is openness and candor. There are no secrets between friends. Thus, I write these lines in all candor and openness. I wish to share with the sisters my innermost thoughts, deepest feelings and the secret aspirations of my soul at this critical juncture in my life. I do this in the hope that this sharing will be a source of grace to the sisters, will bring us all closer to our one and only true friend, Jesus Christ, and will be a spiritual memento when I am no longer here.

In one of his letters, St. Paul writes, "Say only those things which are useful to hear." These words express not only divine wisdom but good common sense as well. Thus, I will try to write only about those things which I feel are beneficial, positive and useful for the reader.

I will limit myself, more or less, to the last three years of my life, beginning with the onset of ALS. But the last three years of my life are the sum total of the 57 years or so which preceded them. By focusing on the final three years, I will, in effect, be writing the story of my entire life. I write in the light of faith and will try to concentrate mostly on the spiritual dimensions and meaning of what I choose to reveal and discuss.

I will not write too much about my faults, failures, mistakes or sins — although these are many indeed. I see no purpose in doing so. Such an exercise, I believe, would hardly be edifying and would simply embarrass the reader and make him or her a helpless victim of my humility. Although St. Augustine, St. Paul, St. Margaret Mary, St. Catherine of Siena and St. Therese of Lisieux and many, many others wrote about their failures with great humility and even enthusiasm and joy, I have decided, at least in these pages, not to emulate them.

As mentioned previously, I am writing this book, first and foremost, for the Sisters of Mary, my daughters and friends in Christ. Secondly, I am writing this book for myself. It is a form of personal prayer in which I hope to express praise and thanksgiving and give glory to God for all His gifts, graces and blessings, not the least of which is my current illness. Also, I think it will be a form of personal therapy and catharsis. It helps on occasion to exteriorize the inner pain and to articulate anguish which you feel in the depths of your soul. Moreover, writing these lines should help me to clarify my thinking and assist me in making a very important decision concerning the future and how I should handle this ALS disease with which I am now afflicted.

The normal time frame of ALS from diagnosis to death as mentioned above is three years, but the time of death can be pushed back indefinitely if one opts for certain extraordinary medical procedures. These medical procedures in our present day and age, although they are not normal, are really not sophisticated or complicated. They involve two operations. The first is a tracheostomy, which entails surgically making an opening through the neck into the windpipe. A tube may then be inserted into the opening so that oxygen can be delivered by a ventilator or respirator. The second operation is called a gastrostomy. It involves making a hole in the stomach by cutting through the abdominal wall and into the stomach wall and suturing the two walls together. A plastic tube is pushed through the abdominal and stomach walls so that the patient can receive fluids and nutrients through it.

Normally, an ALS patient, in the final stages of illness can no longer speak. However, the eye muscles are never affected by the disease. In the last five or ten years, technicians have developed sophisticated computers with voice synthesizers which can be activated by simply winking and blinking your eyes. The good news is that, even if you are on life-support systems, breathing through a tube in your throat and eating through a tube in your stomach, you can still communicate with the outside world. I personally feel a certain revulsion at the thought of being hooked up to these life-support systems. The idea of lying there, totally paralyzed, breathing through a hole in your throat, eating through a tube in your stomach and speaking through a computer by winking and blinking your eyes, holds little appeal for me. My gut instinct at this point in time, although it is quite possible that later I may change my mind, is to let nature take its course and to accept death without trying to outwit it by any extraordinary means.

Some ALS patients who are on life-support systems are held up as heroes. They are spoken about as models of courage, determination and as having the will to live. This is one point of view.

An equally strong case can be made for the opposite. It can be argued that it is just as courageous, heroic and noble to accept death with calm, dignity and serenity as it is to accept a prolonged illness and disability with the same calm, dignity and serenity.

However, those closest to me, namely, the Sisters of Mary, all seem to feel rather strongly that I should hang on to life as long as possible, even though I am hanging only by my fingernails. They even make me feel, at times, that to choose a different course could somehow be interpreted as being a coward.

The heart of the issue, however, is not what I want nor what the sisters want nor, for that matter, what anyone else wants. The real question is what does the Lord want? In this spirit, St. Paul writes, "Whether I live, I live for the Lord; whether I die, I die for the Lord. Whether I live, whether I die, I am the Lord's."

My hope is, by articulating my thoughts and verbalizing my inmost feelings, I will be better able to reach a conclusion and make a lucid decision concerning this important question.

There is one more reservation I have in beginning this undertaking. In Scripture it is written, "Where there are many words, there are many sins." There will be many words in this book. By the same token, there will be many inadvertent sins against charity, humility and, on occasion, perhaps truth itself. These will not be deliberate and thus, I feel they will in no way offend the Lord. However, I ask for His forgiveness and understanding before beginning this book.

So here I am at the river's edge. The water looks cold, dark and deep. The current seems swift and the distance to the other side seems very far indeed. Still, I hear a voice calling in the night, "Come, come to me." St. Peter heard this voice in the storm on the lake and he responded. However, he didn't make it to the source of the voice. His faith failed him and he slipped and began to sink and perish beneath the waves. I begin this journey of faith and I hope my faith will sustain me so that I make it successfully to the opposite shore where I feel Christ is waiting and calling me and will receive me in His open arms and loving embrace.

Chapter 2

Sister Vincent

S ister Vincent was one of my most beautiful daughters — in a spiritual sense. She was also a very good friend and a model Sister of Mary. I miss her.

Sister Vincent grew up in a farming district near Seoul, Korea. Because of the poor financial situation of her family, she managed to receive only a middle school education. At an early age, she began working in a factory. She quickly developed habits of hard-work, self-sacrifice, and self-denial.

Although the hours she spent in the factory were long and hard, she still remained very active in church work. At first, she was a zealous member of the Legion of Mary. Later, she joined the Young Christian Workers and was an active member of this very apostolic, catholic-action group.

In 1968 or so — I am not very good at dates and those that are recorded in these pages are at best very uncertain — at the age of 21, Sister Vincent joined the Sisters of Mary which was founded only four or five years earlier. She spent about twenty years of her life as a Sister of Mary. Most of that time she was placed in charge of a family of boys — usually older middle school boys. She was short in stature and young in years but she had a real charisma for handling boys.

She was warm, loving and caring but at the same time, tough, firm, and on occasion, even harsh and severe. In a word, she practiced in an exemplary manner the "tough love" which we advocate at our Boystowns and Girlstowns. Virtue is in the middle. Nothing excessive. By this token, the secret to the virtue of love is found in balance. True love must be patient and also impatient. It must be motherly, that is, warm, gentle and caring, but at the same time, fatherly, that is, firm, tough and no-nonsense. Sister Vincent developed the art of this tough love and balanced virtue.

What is more, her love was very effective and fruitful. The youngsters in her charge respected and admired her and responded to her leadership. Sister Vincent had no interest in winning the hearts of her children for herself because true love does not seek its own interest. Her only goal was to win the hearts of her boys in order to lead them to Jesus, our Savior and Redeemer.

In 1987, at the age of about 41, Sister Vincent began experiencing severe intestinal pain. She rarely complained. She endured her discomfort with remarkable patience.

At times, however, the pain prevented her from sleeping at night. When it was too much for her, she would quietly slip out of the room she was sharing with several other sisters, go to the chapel and kneeling before Jesus in the darkness, try to find release from the pain by shedding quiet tears.

She went to our hospital in Pusan for a physical examination. The doctors listened to her but did not take her too seriously because of the very quiet matter-of-fact way that she spoke of her illness. Also, in defense of our doctors, it must be said that our hospital is set up to handle general surgical patients and does not have specialized facilities nor equipment for more difficult cases, such as cancer. To make a long story short, the doctors misdiagnosed her illness and attributed her symptoms to menopause. They gave her some medication and reassured her that in time the symptoms would go away on their own. The doctors, of course, were wrong. The pain did not go away. On the contrary, it got progressively worse.

In January 1988, following the annual retreat and renewal of vows, Sister Vincent went home for her annual seven-day vacation. During her short vacation, she visited other medical facilities with more sophisticated equipment and more specialized doctors. Here it was discovered that she had advanced cancer of the colon. Quite possibly, if it had been diagnosed sooner it could have been stopped in its tracks and even conquered.

Upon returning to Pusan, the doctors in our hospital did another series of tests to confirm the diagnosis which Sister Vincent had obtained from other medical experts. Our doctors confirmed the new diagnosis. Although they were very embarrassed, they were quite honest in admitting their mistake and apologized sincerely to Sister Vincent and her superiors. Sister Vincent harbored no rancor towards the doctors who failed her when she needed them the most. On the contrary, she smilingly accepted their apologies and reassured them she understood and that it was okay.

The doctors suggested chemotherapy. This, they said, would certainly prolong her life and even extend it indefinitely. We told her that we were more than willing to send her to the Gospel Hospital down the road which specializes in chemotherapy and the treatment of cancer patients. The choice was hers. Sister Vincent refused the chemotherapy. She preferred to die with dignity and saw little purpose in complicating or prolonging her life by chemotherapy. I personally feel that her decision was the right one.

Sister Vincent's condition continued to deteriorate. Eventually, she underwent a colostomy which helped her with some of the physical pain and discomfort but also became a source of embarrassment and daily humiliation. Sister Vincent was given a private room in our hospital which became her permanent base of operations. She continued, almost until her death, every day to climb the mountain behind the hospital to our Middle School Boystown facilities where she would continue to work with her boys. After a while, the climb to the top of the steep mountain was too much for her. At this point in time, two sisters assumed the role of Simon of Cyrene and helped her climb the mountain, one on each side supporting and assisting. I could see them winding their way up to the mountain top from my room. It was at the same time something beautiful and wrenching to watch. She would rest two or three times on a rock by the side of the road and then resume her arduous climb. She reminded me of Jesus falling under the weight of His cross, two or three times, before finally making it to the top of Calvary's hill.

Sister Vincent's face was pallid. Her eyes revealed the pain she was experiencing and they indicated that they clearly saw more pain down the road. It has been said, "If you have a thorn in your flesh and can still smile, you are a hero." By this criterion, Sister was something of a hero. She usually had a smile on her lips although it was a tight, pained and somewhat forced smile. She rarely complained. What is more, she was a source of inspiration to her boys. Her presence among them and her words of faith turned their thoughts towards the mysteries of death, judgment, and eternity in a very healthy, wholesome and positive manner.

On a number of occasions, I visited Sister Vincent in her hospital room. She was always cheerful and smiling, although it was obvious that she was smiling through her pain. One day, I was alone with her in the room. I gave her my blessing. Before leaving, she looked at me and with a brave smile said, "Do not worry nor concern yourself with me. I will endure whatever comes with courage." These words touched my heart and my eyes were wet with tears when I left her room.

Sister Vincent's mind was clear and sharp right up to the end. Her nights were long, sleepless and tedious waits for the dawn. Her days were long hours of pain, inner struggle and constant prayer. The end finally and mercifully came on an evening in early December. I was in Manila when I received a phone call from Sister Sophia in Pusan informing me of Sister Vincent's death. I was very busy in Manila, therefore, I told Sister Sophia that I would not be able to come to Korea for the funeral. However, after seeking the counsel of the Lord in prayer, I called Pusan back. I informed Sister Sophia, that, if I could get a flight, I would leave for Korea the next day and offer the funeral mass for Sister Vincent.

I arrived in Pusan on a Tuesday morning. As I recall it was a clear, cold, sunny December morning. I offered the funeral Mass in the large gymnasium of our Boystown Middle School. I was very glad that I decided to go back to Pusan to offer mass, give the funeral oration and officiate at the interment of Sister Vincent to the cold, hard but sanctified ground.

The funeral liturgy had a festive quality about it. There seemed to emanate from the remains of Sister Vincent in the coffin a sweet spiritual perfume which St. Paul refers to as the "fragrance of Christ." Other holy writers have called this the "odor of sanctity." Whatever, those of us who loved Sister Vincent inhaled this sweet spiritual perfume and it made our hearts happy and our souls light and joyful.

After returning to Manila, I noticed on the bulletin board of one of our Girlstown buildings a pictorial display based on the life of Sister Vincent. On the bulletin board above the pictures, someone had written, "Sister Vincent is now in heaven. Sister Vincent, please pray for us." I suggested to the sister in-charge that these words were unfair to Sister Vincent and that they should be changed. For her sake, we should assume that Sister Vincent was in purgatory and that she needed our prayers. I recommended then that Sister direct the children to pray first for Sister Vincent before they presume to pray to her.

Upon reflection, however, I am not too sure that my recommendation was proper. Looking back and thinking about the life of Sister Vincent, I am convinced that she underwent her purification and had her purgatory on earth. I think she traveled non-stop from death to eternal life, from earth to heaven. I am convinced that she is now numbered among those beautiful souls of whom St. John speaks in his Apocalypse. They are "clothed in white. They have come from the great tribulation and they washed their robes white in the blood of the Lamb." In a word, I believe Sister Vincent is in the ranks of the saints in heaven.

Objectively, if one were to compare the patience, courage and tenacity with which Sister Vincent endured her illness with that of other sick people in our hospitals similarly afflicted, one would judge Sister Vincent to be simply average. There are many women from the ranks of the poor who have exhibited outstanding patience, courage, and determination in the face of great suffering and pain. These women were born in poverty and reared in destitution. They married early. They had many children. They subjected themselves to the will of a demanding husband and the whims of in-laws who were dictatorial. Because of malnutrition, overwork and poor hygiene, these women were often ailing and sick. They had little possibility of obtaining proper medical care or treatment.

11

Their only medicine was to endure. They learned early in life that the only way to handle pain was to ignore it. Experience taught them, that, the only way to survive was to accept it without complaining. After a while, they developed truly remarkable patience.

When afflicted with a great illness, such as the cancer which eventually caused the death of Sister Vincent, they endured it in silence with extraordinary patience and heroic courage. If these women — and their number is legion — were members of some religious community, they would be greatly admired and talked about. Their virtue would be extolled because nothing is more impressive, dramatic, and admirable than enduring great suffering and pain with patience and facing death with courage. After death, they would most likely be recommended for canonization.

It is really quite difficult for a sister who has not had benefit of this prior experience and previous training in the school of patience to compete on equal terms with these other unsung heroes and hidden champions. Along these same lines, if holiness were simply patience and courage, then many of the North American Indians who were pagans and even, on some occasions, satanists, would be numbered among the ranks of the canonized saints. Many of these Indians were brought up in a culture of pain and patience and in a tradition of suffering and courage. They were taught to practice self-mastery. They learned quickly how to endure excruciating pain and horrible torture with total serenity. Few priests, sisters, or for that matter, even many canonized saints, could equal the stoic endurance of some of these pagan savages. This was almost purely the work of nature and personal will. Grace had little, if any, part to play in the development of these extraordinary, natural virtues and qualities.

To be perfectly honest, however, Sister Vincent would not be a candidate for canonization because of her patience and courage alone. There were times when her patience grew thin and her courage failed her. She would cry out in pain. She would have lapses of self-pity and, on occasion, when the agony was simply too much for her, she tore pitifully at her bed clothing. However, consider Jesus in the garden of Gethsemane, lying on the ground, trembling, sweating blood, depressed and without strength. He prays that the coming suffering will be diverted. He looks rather pitiful and even weak. But in imitation of Jesus, Sister Vincent, at all times struggled, did her very best and with the help of grace did endure until the end with patience and courage in a very remarkable manner.

However, according to the teachings of Christ, holiness is above all, charity. St. John of the Cross writes, "On the last day, we will be judged by love." In the twenty-fifth chapter of St. Matthew's Gospel, Christ in effect, says the same thing. "On the last day," says Christ, "the Son of Man will separate the just from the unjust as a shepherd who separates sheep from goats." The sheep (those who are in the ranks of the saints) are on the right. The criteria of judgment will be charity, love and service. Jesus will say to those on the right, "Come, blessed of my Father, receive the kingdom prepared for you from the beginning. I was hungry, thirsty, naked, homeless, sick, imprisoned ... and you fed, clothed, sheltered, comforted, and helped me. Amen, Amen, I say to you, as long as you did it to one of these the least of my brothers you did it to me."

In the beautiful story of the Good Samaritan, Jesus expounds the same doctrine. If you love and help your neighbor as did the Good Samaritan who loved and helped the man set upon by robbers, you will also receive, says Jesus, eternal life, happiness and a crown of glory. In this spirit, St. Paul says, "Charity is the bond of perfection," and again, "Above all else, my brothers, have charity." St. Paul speaks of charity as the greatest and most desirable and most precious of charisms. It is even greater than the charism to speak in tongues, heal the sick, teach with power and authority, and perform other visible and dramatic miracles.

Sister Vincent received the charism of charity at an early age. She gave witness to the spirit of love in her heart in an extraordinary manner. Her entire life was devoted to the service of others. She sought only the interest of Christ in the poor, underprivileged, abandoned children entrusted to her. In a figurative sense, she gave her blood and gave her life for Christ through the children as the good shepherd gives his life for his sheep. She looked at her children with the eyes of faith and said to them, in her heart, as Christ said to his disciples at the Last Supper, "Take and eat, this

13

is my body which is given up for you. Take and drink, this is my blood poured out for you."

By this criterion of charity, therefore, I truly believe that Sister Vincent can be spoken of as a saint in heaven. What is more, if the Sisters of Mary were willing to put forth the money, the effort and the time to advance her cause, after a number of years, it is quite possible that we could succeed in having Sister Vincent beatified and even canonized. Why not? I am convinced that there are people of lesser virtue who have been beatified and canonized.

It might be said that one needs authenticated miracles before someone can be declared a saint. I'm not sure what the present requirements are, but if I'm not mistaken, at one time, four authenticated miracles were required for canonization. Here again, I might be completely wrong but I think, if you get enough people praying, making novenas, and using relics in enough places and for a sufficient period of time, you eventually will come up with the necessary documented miracles.

Miracles are not all that rare. In every hospital in the world, during the course of a year of treating, caring for and operating on many patients with different ailments, there are always three or four inexplicable medical phenomena, which could be termed "miracles." That is to say there are patients who have an incurable illness which suddenly disappears and is cured. If these phenomena occur in a civilian hospital, those who work in the hospital accept it with a certain amount of wonder and surprise, but they dismiss it as one of those things in life which has no rational explanation. They shrug their shoulders and think no more about it.

However, if one of these "miracles" happens in a Catholic hospital, and especially, in a setting where there are special prayers, novenas, and blessings and the use of many relics, immediately the same inexplicable medical phenomenon is declared a miracle of God. And well it may be. Because certainly there are miracles of God and I would be a heretic to deny it. In the Gospel, Jesus manifests His power to perform miracles. Many of the saints had miraculous powers of healing. Today, through their intercession, and at certain shrines of Mary, there are real and dramatic interventions of God in the workings of nature and through authentic miracles. But at the same time it must be accepted that we are in a rather vague and nebulous area here. And the point I wish to make is, if you are persistent, clever, and determined enough, the problem of three or four authenticated miracles to back up the process of beatification or canonization is not an overwhelming problem. Upon listening to what I am saying, it sounds a bit blase or cynical and it should be much better nuanced. But this is my honest feeling, so I let it stand as is.

After Sister Vincent's death, I suggested to the sisters that we ask for a sign or a miracle of grace to prove that she was indeed with the saints in heaven. This would strengthen our faith and stimulate us to follow her example of self-sacrifice, courage and charity. The sign or miracle we should ask for, I suggested, was a miracle of charity. If by Easter, I said, there was a definite increase in community charity and the intensity of our brotherly love, we would attribute this grace to the intercession of Sister Vincent and conclude that she was indeed with God.

At Easter, we did a study and made a survey of sorts. Being as objective and unbiased as possible, we all agreed that indeed there was a marked increase in the intensity of charity and a true growth as a community in the virtue of brotherly love. Thus we concluded that Sister Vincent was indeed with God in heaven. Now with total conviction, instead of praying for Sister Vincent as I suggested at first, I suggested that we pray to her.

After the death of Sister Vincent, I personally became aware of her presence in my life. It is difficult to express this, but it is not a question of auto-suggestion, self-delusion, or mere sentimentalism. It is a real, deep, delightful experience of a close, intimate, loving presence which becomes a source of strength, grace and consolation. I have had similar experiences on many other occasions.

I have always felt the loving presence of Christ in my life. It is something very deep, subtle, and usually barely discernible, but it is very real and very precious. Also, in a similar manner, I have experienced the presence of Mary as a loving Mother and an intimate friend. At other times, I have experienced the presence of St. Therese of Lisieux for whom I have a special affection and whom I feel is truly the "soeur de mon ame," the sister of my soul.

I've also experienced the presence of Sister Gertrude, my Carmelite friend and spiritual sponsor for more than thirty years who died just a few months ago. Sister Vincent is another.

Shortly after the death of Sister Vincent, I believe she obtained not only the grace of charity for the Sisters of Mary as a community but she also gave me a special grace. This grace has a name which I mentioned in the previous chapter. It is called amyotrophic lateral sclerosis (ALS), which of course is the terminal illness which is slowly and softly paralyzing and killing me.

Looking back, I believe that this illness began manifesting its presence in my system shortly after the demise of Sister Vincent. I was never wont to monitor my body very closely, so I might be mistaken. But it seems to me, about that time, there were muscular fibrillations or fasciculations, especially in my legs which became more and more noticeable. After my noon-day run and workout, I would look at my legs and wonder why my muscles were trembling, fibrillating, and fasciculating like they were little Mexican jumping beans just under the surface of the skin. I paid little attention to these symptoms and shrugged them off. I did not realize that this is the hallmark of ALS and probably announced the onset of the disease.

If Sister Vincent has obtained for me the grace of this illness, I look to her to obtain for me the grace to endure it with patience, courage, and determination. After Sister Vincent died, I thought back upon her life and reflected upon her illness. I wondered if I could endure such pain with similar patience. I concluded that I could not and in no way could I match her patience and courage. After two or three years of fighting ALS, I still feel the same. But I am sure that this loving daughter and good, close friend in Jesus will obtain for me the patience, the courage, the determination to endure whatever comes and to endure it with a smile.

In the early stages of this illness, I prayed that it might go into remission and burn out as it frequently does. It frequently reaches a plateau and then just stays there indefinitely. I felt there was so much more I would like to do and could do for the glory of God, that even though I was severely disabled I would be happy to continue. Others have prayed fervently for full, complete and miraculous recovery. Now my prayer is limited to two intentions.

First, I wish to die a happy death, a death of love, such as did St. Therese of Lisieux and Sister Vincent. A death of love is one which is quiet, calm, and death with a smile. Second, I would like to follow the example and path of Sister Vincent and go non-stop from earth to heaven without any delays in purgatory. So, I entrust these two intentions to Sister Vincent and I'm sure she will obtain them for me.

Chapter 3

The Beginning

"Some deadly thing has fastened on to my body," writes a psalmist. Some deadly thing has fastened itself on my body and has been hidden in my system for some time now. As mentioned before, the light muscular fibrillations in my legs hinted at the presence of this deadly thing.

However, what happened one night in July 1989 was much more than a subtle hint. It was a dramatic announcement that left little doubt that something serious was taking place in my body.

I woke up in the middle of the night with a strange sensation in the biceps of my right arm. They were twitching, fasciculating or fibrillating with great gusto. What is more, the fasciculations did not stop. It continued without diminishing as if there were a steady electrical current attached to my muscles. At times, I would look at my right biceps with awe and wonder. I would watch with fascination at the rippling, jumping and twitching that was taking place in this area. As mentioned before, muscular fasciculation of this type is the hallmark of ALS. I did not know it at that time, but it means that the nerves in the spine are being attacked and they are dying. Since the nerves cannot send impulses to the muscles any longer, the muscles cease to be stimulated, and they too atrophy and die with time.

The muscular fasciculation was accompanied by a slow but steady muscular deterioration first noticeable in my right arm. The number of push-ups I could do diminished from twenty to ten, to five, to zero. In the pool, I had great difficulty in getting my right arm over my shoulder and head when I was swimming. Also, there was no power in my pull and stroke with my right arm.

I continued, however, my daily runs as I had been doing for almost twenty-five years. Running was such an integral part of my daily living that I did not know how I could survive without it. I was addicted to running in a positive sense just as a heavy smoker shrinks and trembles at the thought of giving up nicotine, and a heavy drinker is filled with terror at the thought of never taking another drink. I was frightened by the idea of never being able to run again.

Running was such a marvelous release for me. It was great therapy. At the same time, the increase of oxygen to the brain stimulated the creative process and helped greatly to resolve problems and solve difficulties that were troubling me. Running also gave me a healthy high. The surcharge of endorphins relaxed and refreshed me.

Every day, for almost twenty-five years, rain or shine, no matter what part of the world I found myself, I would go out for a daily run and work-out. Normally, I would interrupt my work at noon, change clothes, go out for a run for an hour or at times much more. Then I would return to my room, shower and eat lunch, usually a cheese or peanut butter sandwich, washed down with a glass of Tang. Then I would rest for twenty or thirty minutes before beginning the afternoon's activities.

Although I continued my running, I reduced somewhat the pace and time, not so much in deference to the muscular fasciculation that I noticed especially in my right biceps but mostly because I was having increasing difficulty with my right leg. In a high school football accident, I badly fractured my right ankle and greatly weakened that side of my body. I believe this led to the severe arthritis in my right hip and shoulder that I was experiencing. Although running was painful, it was more painful not to run. I struck a balance and concluded that although I might be harming my body, the psychological and emotional and spiritual benefit compensated for this.

Usually, I would prepare to run by first massaging my right leg with ice. I would massage it with ice again, after completing the run, then again, before I went to bed at night, if the leg were causing me too much discomfort. Sounds a little crazy, doesn't it? But, sports fans, I'm afraid that's the way I am — or to be more exact, that's the way I was.

The muscle fasciculation could hardly be ignored and it kept reminding me that something — maybe something quite serious — was the matter with my body, and, perhaps, I should look into the matter. At the time this was happening, I was very much involved with construction of our new Boystown/Girlstown complex in Cebu in the Philippines. I was going back and forth by plane on a frequent basis to supervise the building and to help with the planning.

I returned to Korea in early September. Immediately, I tried to find a sports physician — that is, a doctor who himself was an athlete and understood the problems of athletes. I felt he would be more in tune with my difficulties and would be better able to advise and assist me.

After a little detective work, Damiano Park, my Korean man-Friday of twenty-five years or more, located the head of the newly-formed Sports Medicine Department of Korea. The surgeon in charge was an orthopedic doctor. He agreed to see me in his office at seven-thirty in the morning. He was cheerful, pleasant and very confident of his diagnosis after a rather perfunctory examination. He pronounced with authority that my problem was in no way neurological but simply muscular. It was due to excessive physical activity while being dehydrated and was a result of a loss of magnesium. He gave me the brand name of some magnesium pills. All I had to do was take these on a regular basis and presto, the problem would disappear.

Although he did not know what he was talking about, he did it with such confidence and cheerfulness that I returned to our Boystown feeling rather elated. It was about noon and I went out for a run and enjoyed it more than ever, now that I knew my problem had been diagnosed and the cure had been prescribed. However, the magnesium pills which I began taking had no effect whatsoever.

It was now early October in Korea and the International Eucharistic Congress was in full swing. The Pope attended, as did the Bishops and representatives from all over the world, including those from the Philippines.

On succeeding days, we had various distinguished members of the Filipino hierarchy visit our Boystown, offer Mass for the children and speak to them. First on the list was Cardinal Sin from Manila. The next day was Cardinal Vidal's turn. Two days later, Archbishop Legazpi, who was then president of the Bishop's Conference of the Philippines, came for Mass, breakfast and a tour of our facilities.

On Friday, October 6, I took a delegation of Filipino bishops including Cardinal Sin, Cardinal Vidal, Archbishop Legazpi, Bishop Quirino and one or two of their aides to Pusan. Bishop Lee, the ordinary of Pusan, was waiting at our Boystown to graciously greet our guests from the Philippines.

The occasion for the visit was the blessing and inauguration of the new million dollar Girlstown building which had just been completed. After a blessing ceremony, a tour of the facilities and a concelebrated Mass attended by all the children, we retired to the Boystown building where a simple lunch had been prepared.

After lunch, the bishops attended a sparkling, enthusiastic, musical program prepared by the children and the sisters. It was really a marvelous day and one of those beautiful memories you store in the back of your mind and pull out later when things get tough.

Everyone was impressed by the children and the sisters. The praise by the visitors was lavish. Cardinal Vidal, for example, kept repeating, "The sisters seem so fervent and yet so simple. Really, they are exactly what the Church in the Philippines needs." Cardinal Sin remarked, "These are very highly-motivated women." Archbishop Legazpi was equally positive in his remarks and he was quite effusive in his evaluations of our program for the 2,000 handicapped street people at Kaengsaengwon in Seoul. Archbishop Legazpi confided in me he had three secret wishes. He wanted me to bring my sisters to his Archdiocese of Naga and 1) build a Boystown/Girlstown complex, 2) begin a program for destitute TB patients and 3) start a program for destitute mentally-ill people.

Archbishop Legazpi visited our Boystown in Seoul on October 7, 1989 the feast of Our Lady of the Rosary. Being a Dominican, he has a special devotion to Our Lady of the Rosary. On that day, he gave me a beautiful rosary as a gift and a personal memento. He said that it had been his practice to give a rosary on that day to some friend or special person and I was the special person for that particular year.

During the visit to Pusan, I spotted Cardinal Sin and Bishop Lee in a corner engaged in an intense and serious discussion. I discreetly looked away because Cardinal Sin had given me a hint as to the nature of the discussion. He had informed me during our breakfast meeting at the Boystown in Seoul, two days earlier, that he had decided to make me an honorary prelate (monsignor). In order to present this request to Rome, it was essential that he obtain the permission of Bishop Lee, my superior and ordinary.

Cardinal Sin never inquired concerning my wishes, that is, whether or not I wanted to become a monsignor. But he made up his own mind and he was pursuing this purpose with charm, persuasiveness and intensity. I knew he was talking to Bishop Lee about his plans and trying to cajole Bishop Lee into consenting. I shook my head and said to myself, there is no way Bishop Lee will consent. However, I underestimated the prowess and powers of persuasion of Cardinal Sin. Upon returning to Seoul, the Cardinal announced that he had obtained Bishop Lee's permission and was ready to move ahead with the petition for monsignorship.

After Cardinal Sin's departure from Korea, I considered writing him a polite letter saying, "Thanks, but no thanks." I was not very attracted to the title of monsignor. I was very happy to live and die as simply, Father. But then I hesitated concerning the letter. First, I thought, this thing will never go through. Either Rome will turn down the request, or else, the documents will come back for Bishop Lee's signature. By that time, he will have regained his senses and simply put the papers in a drawer and forgotten about them. In due time, this whole idea will dissolve and disappear. Also, I thought that if I wrote such a letter to Cardinal Sin, he might be needlessly offended. So I decided to do nothing and put the matter out of my mind.

However, the matter did not dissolve nor go up in smoke. To my surprise, it went right through and word came from Korea that

Rome had signed all the documents and upon my return to the Philippines, there would be an investiture ceremony. But this is for a subsequent, exciting chapter.

Chapter 4

The Diagnosis

I arrived in Washington towards the end of October in 1989. Arrangements had been made for me to stay with the Carmelite Fathers on Lincoln Road, a change from my customary habit of staying in a motel near our office during my visits to the United States. During this visit, however, I felt I needed a spiritual environment. So I asked the Carmelites through Bill Vita, my brother-in-law, for their hospitality and they graciously complied. As it turned out, this was a happy decision and the arrangements were providential.

At seven o'clock sharp on the morning after my arrival, I had my first medical appointment with an internist. I had been having a lot of trouble with my gastrointestinal tract. I had problems with my GI tract all my life, but of late they were more frequent and severe. The internist examined me, ran some tests and then prescribed medication, which, to my surprise, turned out to be quite effective — at least for awhile.

My next appointment was with a famous orthopedic surgeon among whose patients were many famous athletes. It was his turn to work me over. He ordered a series of x-rays and after examining them, told me that I needed two operations, one on my shoulder and a second on my right hip. "That hip is crying out for help," he said. In fact, the arthritis in my right hip was so bad that nothing short of a complete replacement would do the job. As an afterthought, the doctor added, "No more running or jogging. You can work out a little on a bicycle and you can swim, but, running and jogging are out." These words were like a death sentence and struck terror in my heart.

My final medical appointment for the day was with a podiatrist. He looked at my right foot, ankle and hip, gave me advice on how to relieve the pain, what shoes to wear and so on. I asked if my years of running were the cause of the arthritis with which I had just been diagnosed. He said there are two theories. One, running causes arthritis. The second is the opposite, that running prevents arthritis. "Either way," he said, "you would have gotten it, eventually."

I was in a quandary about the advice from the orthopedic surgeon. He was recommending not one, but two major operations that would put me out of action for a period of three to six months including post-operative physical therapy. I was not ready to stay in the U.S. for such an extended period of time. What to do? A quick decision was called for and I made it.

I went back to see my orthopedic surgeon and told him, "Let's get on with it and make plans for the necessary surgery." He said he would do nothing until I had received a thorough neurological work-up because of the disturbing fasciculation in my arm muscles. I asked him to refer me to a neurologist. Immediately he called up Dr. Korengold who has facilities on Wisconsin Avenue. I saw Dr. Korengold the next day. The tests in his office indicated that not only was my right arm very weak but there was a marked weakness in my left arm also. He immediately arranged for me to have a sophisticated electrical examination. As I recall, I lay on a table in a dark room. Two or three technicians with computers all around them put needles in various parts of my body. A doctor came in to supervise the proceedings. They measured electrical impulses by computer to try to determine if there was anything wrong with my neurological system. The test seemed interminable. At the beginning there was a lot of light banter and joking between the doctor, the technicians and myself. But as the test proceeded, the joking and the bantering ceased. The atmosphere grew a bit tense and heavy. I sensed they had discovered a serious anomaly. When the test was concluded, I said to the doctor, "Something is quite wrong, isn't it?" He nodded his head without comment.

Dr. Korengold made arrangements for additional tests. I didn't realize it at that time but the diagnosis of ALS is reached by a process of elimination. There are twenty-seven varieties of diseases that could cause similar symptoms. The way to arrive at ALS is to eliminate all the other possibilities and bingo! you are left with the only alternative which is ALS. Among the many tests which Dr. Korengold conducted was a spinal tap. This was followed by a Magnetic Resonance Imagery (MRI) which is a very interesting type of examination. The machine itself costs in the neighborhood of four million dollars. The patient is slid into the machine and it is almost like they are being entombed or encapsulated. I didn't mind all these tests. In fact, I found them interesting, even a bit fascinating and enjoyable.

Dr. Korengold shocked me by asking my consent to give me a test for AIDS. He said this was standard medical procedure. The results of these tests, however, were negative.

During my brief stay in the U.S., I saw a series of very distinguished doctors in a very short period of time. I was greatly impressed by their competence and professionalism, but above all, by their kindness. Most of the doctors are very well-known in their fields and their fees are usually very, very hefty. But almost without exception, they gave me their services free of charge. This touched and impressed me.

I went back to see Dr. Korengold for the final verdict. I was in the waiting room with Bill Vita when the doctor came in. He looked serious, even agitated and asked if I desired Bill Vita to accompany me into his office. Immediately, I realized what he had to say was quite serious. I said it was not necessary for Bill to be with me.

The doctor explained, that, looking at all the material and test results, there was a better than a fifty-percent chance that I had what is called amyotrophic lateral sclerosis (ALS), a motor neuron disease or, more popularly, Lou Gehrig's disease. I asked, "Is the disease life-threatening?" He answered, "Yes, it is. The usual period of time is three years." But immediately he added that he had known someone who had lived with the disease for as long as seven years.

He gave me the name, address and telephone number of a

famous ALS specialist in San Francisco, Dr. Forbes Norris. He urged me to stop by San Francisco on my way back to Korea to see Dr. Norris in order to confirm his diagnosis. Dr. Korengold said, "Truly, I hope I am wrong."

I left Dr. Korengold's office with a pamphlet concerning the disease which apparently was now doing its work in my body. The title of the pamphlet was Amyotrophic Lateral Sclerosis (ALS) — which is another name for motor neuron disease. I laughed aloud. I was in the car with Bill Vita. I said, "Can you believe it? This disease ALS has my name on it." Frequently, I would sign my name Al S. in place of Al Schwartz. Apparently, we two — that is, amyotrophic lateral sclerosis (ALS) and yours truly, AL S. — were destined for each other.

Like most people, I knew little about ALS. I like the sound of "Lou Gehrig's disease." It has a strong, masculine, athletic ring to it. I vaguely remember the movie in which Gary Cooper played the role of Lou Gehrig. It was called "Pride of the Yankees." Lou Gehrig was a famous baseball player, second only to Babe Ruth. At the height of his career in 1939, he contracted ALS and died of it two years later in 1941. The movie ends with a glorious tribute to Lou Gehrig in Yankee Stadium. He walks very stiffly and carefully across the field to the microphone. He gives a speech in which he says, "I think I am the luckiest man alive." The crowd erupts with applause and rises to its feet. Lou Gehrig walks heroically out of the stadium into the dug-out tunnel with the roar of the crowd ringing in his ears.

In the back of my mind I said, "What a beautiful way to go, so glorious and heroic." Of course, all this was sentimental nonsense.

I read some of the medical literature concerning the disease. Two words in the literature describing the disease stuck in my mind. These two words were "cruel" and "demeaning." I really did not know what these words meant at that time. Now, two and a half years later, I know.

As mentioned previously, I was staying with the Carmelite Fathers at that time. I was doing a lot of praying and reflecting. This was the most community life I had experienced since leaving the seminary over thirty years before and I was enjoying the hospitality and camaraderie.

In front of the monastery there is a beautiful cemetery and park called Lincoln Park. The trees were turning gold in the autumn light. Every day I would take light runs through the cemetery. It was such a beautiful, even mystical experience that it is difficult to describe. The beauty, the silence, the softness, the solitude and the presence of the dead, all created an atmosphere extremely conducive to contemplation. As I ran along the roads, looking at the tombs and the trees and the light and the beautiful sky, I thought of death, not in a morbid manner, but with a certain calm, serenity and even joy. In my heart I felt that these were my last runs and very soon I would not be able to enjoy this experience.

I was in the U.S. not much more than a total of three weeks in all. There was a certain deep peace, inner joy and spiritual happiness associated with this particular visit. It was as if I was on a spiritual high. I had experienced similar highs on other occasions in my life. Something in me hinted that this was the cloud of glory which surrounded Jesus and His apostles on Mount Tabor which in turn was a preparation for the night of Gethsemane and the darkness of Calvary.

St. Thomas Aquinas wrote, "Man cannot live without happiness." God knows of what man is made, that he is made only of dust and clay. So he knows we cannot make it without happiness. He gives us the happiness in the right amount, the right kind, the right dosage, sometimes before, sometimes after, sometimes during the trials and tribulations we suffer. But He always gives just enough to keep us going. The happiness I was experiencing during my stay in the U.S. is difficult to describe, but it has kept me going for many a month and has still not been fully exhausted.

During my stay with the Carmelite Fathers, I turned off the lights in my room and was preparing for bed as is my custom. I was changing into my pajamas in a semi-darkened room. I don't know how it happened, but suddenly, I lost my balance and fell. I didn't realize it at the time, but this was ALS at work. This was the first of a series of five or six very bad falls triggered by the disease.

I reached out instinctively to protect myself as I fell. To my amazement I opened a wooden panel on the side of the wall. I had seen the panel by the bed but did not know what it was. Now it was open. I was lying on the floor looking through a plate glass window at the chapel below. The chapel was darkened. I could see the vigil light flickering and could see distinctly the altar and the tabernacle. I had not known it but the Fathers put me in a room reserved for sick priests. During Mass the panel is opened and the priest staying in the room can assist at Mass and adore the Blessed Sacrament from his sick room. I lay on the floor a bit shaken and bruised, looking at the chapel, the flickering red light and the tabernacle glowing in the soft light. I said to myself, "Sacerdos et Victima, Priest and Victim." This was Jesus. This was the call of every alter Christus. So I said in my heart, "Lord, if that is what you want, here I am. I offer myself as a victim to Your Love." I knew St. Therese had offered herself as a victim to Divine Love and encouraged many "little souls" to follow her example. I took this occasion to mouth these words and speak this prayer, not fully realizing the implication of what I was saying. If at that time I knew what lay ahead, I am not sure I would have spoken these words so easily and so swiftly.

Also, during my stay with the Carmelite Fathers, something else of a providential nature occurred. I had one morning with nothing on my schedule. No doctors' appointments, no tests, no meetings, nothing. So after Mass and breakfast, I decided to spend the morning, and if possible the entire day, in recollection, spiritual reading, prayer and meditation. I was sitting in my room with a pad of paper making a tentative schedule for the day. There was a soft knock at the door. "Come in," I shouted, "the door is open." To my surprise, Father Jose from Venezuela entered and smilingly asked if he could chat with me a bit. He was a medical doctor before entering the Carmelites. He was in the U.S. to perfect his English. I had seen him at the monastery every day. We had smiled and greeted each other but we had never really engaged in conversation. Every day, he explained to me, he would go to the English Institute and return late at night. This morning, however, he said he had contracted a bad cold and for the first time since his visit to the U.S. he could not go to school. For some reason or another, he said, he felt he should come to see me and to talk to me. He began talking about his plans for a "Carmelite City" in the mountains of Venezuela. I was impressed by his deep faith, sincerity and apostolic zeal.

I explained a bit about the work I was involved in and the programs and projects I had started. He listened intently then became very moved and spoke with conviction. He said such programs and projects were greatly needed in Venezuela. He insisted that I come to Caracas and start our Boystown and Girlstown there. He had many contacts among the clergy, even the hierarchy and people of power and means. He assured me he would do his very best to help me. He said he felt the presence of the Holy Spirit in the room and he was convinced that it was the Holy Spirit who had guided him to me and that it was the Holy Spirit who wanted to lead me to South America.

I was struck by the coincidence of our meeting and the sincerity of the priest. However, I reserved judgment about whether or not it was the work of the Holy Spirit. In the back of my mind, however, I felt eventually I should begin the Sisters of Mary Boystown and Girlstown programs in a third country. In fact, three years before, when Cardinal Sin suggested he take our constitution to Rome for approval, I demurred. I said, "Thank you, your Eminence. But I prefer to wait until we establish our presence in a third country." With surprise he asked me what country I had in mind. At that time I said maybe India or Mexico. I felt after the work in the Philippines was stabilized and had been consolidated, we could think about a program in a third country. But that was way down the road, maybe five, ten, twenty years hence, certainly, not then.

However, with the diagnosis of ALS, it was clear that my time was very limited and my days were numbered. If I wanted to do anything I would have to act quickly. However, I was not particularly attracted to Venezuela. I had visited Caracas at one time and knew the poverty in the slums of that city. Father Jose said Venezuela was the gateway of Latin America. In fact, Mother Teresa had made her first Latin American foundation in that country. I countered that Mexico would be a logical place to begin, if ever I were to go to South America. He shook his head and said Mexico was too complicated.

Our God is a God of encounters. Looking back I am convinced it was God who arranged this encounter which was the first in a series of encounters which eventually led me to Mexico. I left the U.S. and returned to Korea by way of San Francisco. I had a delightful visit with Dr. Forbes Norris who is a world renowned expert on ALS. He confirmed Dr. Korengold's diagnosis. He gave me some advice. He said those who survived ALS the longest have three things in common. One, a good, positive outlook. Two, they remained physically active as long as possible. Three, they have a good physical constitution at the onset of the disease. Later, an ALS patient added a fourth, namely, faith in God. Of these four requirements for a long survival, I had three, namely, a good, positive mental outlook; I was physically active and had a strong faith. As for the solid, physical constitution, this was at best questionable. So the great battle with ALS had been engaged. I returned to Korea with my disease, the inner spiritual glow still very much alive and my fasciculating muscles reminding me and warning me that the future was going to be very difficult indeed.

Chapter 5

Long Day's Journey into Night

It is always a mistake to underestimate one's opponent. I have been guilty of just such a mistake with regards to ALS.

After being diagnosed with this disease, I read all the available medical literature I could get my hands on. The literature describes ALS as an illness which is "terminal" and also "very cruel and demeaning." What is more the disease usually proceeds at a slow, steady but inexorable pace. These words sound ominous enough but for some reason or other I did not fully grasp their meaning. I knew ALS was no joke but at the same time I felt that with God's grace I could handle it, and I tended to treat it somewhat lightly.

Now after two years with this disease I realize that ALS is no lightweight. It is a real heavyweight, and if the truth must be told, at times I feel that I am taking one hell of a beating.

I feel like I have been pushed into the ring to do battle with Mike Tyson. Mike Tyson weighs in at about 230 pounds, and I now weigh about 112 pounds. Clearly this is a mismatch.

Mike has been given instructions not to put me away until the final seconds of the fifteenth and last round. Until then, he is free to batter me, beat-up on me, pummel me, and play with me to his heart's content. Occasionally, I glance rather helplessly at the people in my corner, suggesting with my eyes that they throw in the towel. Whenever I do this, they either look down or look the other way and ignore my silent plea. Occasionally, when Mike gets particularly ferocious the referee steps in between mighty

Mike and little me, and peers intently into my eyes to see if they are clear enough to keep the fight going. I look back into the referee's eyes silently pleading with him to stop the fight. But, after a second or two, he jumps aside and with the wave of his hand signals that the fight is to continue. If it were up to me, I would gladly drop to the canvas and lay there for the count of ten. But Mike has me on the ropes and his battering fists and the ropes keep me erect. So, even if I want to, I cannot go down.

Between each round there is a period of rest and refreshment. God always gives us these breathing spaces. So, between rounds, I get a cold drink, my trainers wash me off and wipe me down, and whisper encouraging and consoling words. Then the mouthpiece is put back in my mouth, the bell sounds, and I am pushed out into the ring for another round.

At this point in the compilation of this book, I am having serious second thoughts. I hear a little voice deep inside asking the question, is it really worth the effort? Can these words possibly be of any benefit to anyone? Would it not be better to pack it all in, and to abandon this project as an idea whose time has not yet come?

The medical literature on ALS usually states that although the disease kills the nerves and paralyzes the muscles, it leaves the mental faculties intact. The mind remains sharp, the imagination creative, and the memory remains clear and focused at all times.

Not long ago, in the company of two of my sisters, I visited a Filipino woman in Manila who, although only about 42, has been suffering from ALS for ten years or so. Since that visit I have learned that she has passed away. However, at that time she stated that her personal experience confirmed what the medical experts propound. She said, if anything, she felt that her mind and memory were more alert, active and alive than before the illness.

My experience has been somewhat different. A frequent problem with ALS is sleep disorder. Many patients suffer from serious insomnia. I am one of these. I find it difficult to get more than three or four hours of restful sleep a night. Although, my body demands and needs something closer to seven or eight hours. In addition to insomnia, another hallmark of ALS is chronic and heavy physical fatigue.

If your body is heavy with fatigue from a lack of adequate

sleep, it stands to reason that your intellectual faculties will also become impaired. I feel that, not only has my physical activity been greatly impaired by the disease, but my intellectual activity now requires a much greater effort than before.

The date on which I am composing these lines is July 15, 1991. It is Monday morning, about nine o'clock. I am sitting before a microphone and a tape recorder in my room on the seventh floor, roof-deck of our recently completed Boystown at Silang, Cavite in the Philippines. I look out the window and see a magnificent landscape of coconut groves with lovely green mountains rising in the distance. A little to the left, I can see the morning sun sparkling and glistening on Laguna Lake.

So, here I sit, looking at this beautiful scenery on the outside and fighting with the temptation on the inside to abandon this idea of an autobiography as a waste of time and an unnecessary burden. But then, I hear another small voice in the back of my mind, "So, give up the book, but then what will you do with the hours of the morning which stretch out before you as a vast, empty wasteland? How will you make it through the morning into the afternoon?" I hear myself answering, "I can always read or study." But the fact is, as almost everything else in my life, reading, too, has become an activity very burdensome and fraught with difficulty.

Not long ago, my office in Washington sent me a very expensive electronic page-turner, but it is something of a disappointment. You activate the gadget by a foot switch or sucking on a tube, like a straw. But it is really a hit or miss operation. Frequently, the gadget misses and the page does not turn. At other times it hits too hard and turns over a half dozen or more pages at one time. I can arrange for one of the sisters to stand at my elbow and serve as my voice-activated page turner. However, it is not very conducive to reflection to have someone standing next to you literally breathing on your neck as you try to ponder the contents of a book.

Well, continues the same little voice, "Why don't you try prayer? You can always spend the hours of the day in meditation and contemplation, as John of the Cross and Teresa of Avila did."

My answer to this is that I have the afternoons and evenings for prayer.

But, more to the point, I am no John of the Cross or Teresa of Avila. I do more praying now than ever before, but, frequently, my prayer is a struggle with sleepiness and fatigue. Prayer becomes another form of struggle and combat albeit spiritual.

Although compiling this book requires a certain amount of effort and involves a certain amount of discomfort and pain, I can only conclude it would be more painful not to work on it. Experience has taught me that I have an extremely low threshold for boredom. For me, boredom is the greatest form of pain. I feel it is important to do my best to remain active and productive as long as possible.

The conclusion to all this inner dialogue is to keep going with the book no matter how difficult. It is a form of therapy. Also, as I mentioned in the introduction, it is a form of prayer — perhaps not the mystical prayer of John of the Cross or Teresa of Avila, but it is a prayer of praise suited to my present condition and circumstances. If I offer this prayer with faith and simplicity, I feel it will give glory to God, be beneficial to my own soul, and perhaps may even be of help to others who read these lines.

At this juncture, I would like to get something else off my chest. Before beginning this chapter I read the transcript of the previous chapters. What I have written sounds pietistic and sanctimonious. I ask myself, do you really believe that this ALS thing is a gift from God and a grace obtained through the intercession of a dear, departed friend and sister? Do you really believe what you were saying when you mouthed the prayer about being a victim, like St. Therese of Lisieux? Are you playing games and trying to kid people? At times you can hardly stand up on your feet and yet you write these beautiful words. Who are you trying to kid? It is obvious that my feelings are ambivalent at best.

But, then too, so were the feelings of Christ in the Garden of Gethsemane. He sweats blood, struggles inwardly, agonizes and is filled with terror and trembling at the thought of the approaching passion, humiliation and death. But, He does not get up and run. The same with Christ on the Cross on Calvary. The inward struggle continues, He is filled with darkness, and He articulates his despair with the pitiful cry, "My God, My God, why have You forsaken Me?" But at the same time He does not come down from the Cross, as he could have easily done.

No, what I have written stands. I have expressed as sincerely and candidly as possible what is in my heart. I have written words which I do not perhaps practice fully, but I wish to practice and live them, and I continue to struggle and do my best. Having gotten this little aside out of the way, let me try to get on with this chapter which promises to be as interminable as ALS itself.

What I had planned to do in this chapter was to describe my daily routine — a day in the life of an ALS patient. Yesterday, Sunday — although not a typical day because of the fact that it was Sunday and a holiday — could serve as an illustration of how I spend my time. Each week I deteriorate and decline as the disease progresses. So, what I write now will be quite different from what I would write one month from now or even one week from now.

Yesterday, I woke up a little after three in the morning, after a night of mediocre rest. I cannot say that I tossed and turned all night, because tossing and turning are luxuries which are denied the ALS patient. You just lie there and do your best to grow quiet and still, relax and rest. My leg hurts and my left shoulder is somewhat painful. My hand is trapped under my leg, and I cannot free it. The room seems very hot. I am perspiring and quite thirsty.

Finally, at 5:15 sharp the long night is over and the door to my room opens. I hear a cheerful "Good morning, Father," from the two sisters who care for me. The sisters get me to the edge of my bed. I sit and my right leg starts doing its morning dance. It is now very spastic and jumps up and down, rather out of control. The sisters help me to my feet. Once again, the right leg becomes very shy and timid and it takes a good deal of coaching to get it to cooperate and straighten up. I must be very cautious, because, if at all possible I must avoid another fall. Already in the course of this illness, I have taken five or six bad falls. Each left me a bit bruised and shaken, but, happily, not seriously hurt. However, another fall at this stage of the illness could be quite serious. If I were to break a bone, it would not heal. If I were to strike my head, it could very well be fatal.

However, the two sisters are both nurses, and they are

becoming more and more adept at handling me. After getting me into the wheelchair, one pushes me to a table on which has been prepared a tape recorder and a cup of coffee with a straw in it. The cup of coffee is placed on top of several books so that the straw touches my lips and I can drink it easily without moving my neck. The muscles in my neck and shoulders are now quite weak, so that if my head drops it just hangs there, limp on my chest. I have great difficulty in getting it back into an upright position. As I begin sipping the coffee, the recorder is turned on, and I listen to the sermon for the children's Mass which I prepared the previous evening. The sermon winds down as I am finishing the cup of coffee. The recorder is switched off and the sisters start getting me ready for Mass.

Right now, I have very little control over my environment. I have lost all independence and so-called dignity. However, I do not find this all that devastating. I think of Jesus, Lord and Master, who had all power in heaven and earth, yet He deigned to become a small infant. He entrusted Himself totally, to the Virgin of Nazareth. She was free to move Him this way or that way, to dress Him or undress Him, bathe Him, wash Him, and so on. Jesus accepts this with calm serenity and total surrender. He does the same in the Eucharist. If the priest puts the host on the left side of the altar, it remains there. If he places it on the right side of the altar, it stays there. The priest has total control of Jesus in the Eucharist as Mary did over Jesus, when He was an infant. This example of my Lord and Master gives me peace and courage. I try to emulate this example and to let go of any inner resistance. In an easy, relaxed manner, I try to simply go with the flow.

The sisters are really angels of mercy. They are patient, caring and very proficient. On this count I consider myself very fortunate. I suffer from no lack of both dedicated and loving people who are not only willing but very anxious to take care of me. I have been told that ALS is so difficult to cope with that many spouses abandon their partners who are afflicted with this disease. I do not know what I would do without these dedicated sisters to look after me.

It takes about a half hour to get me ready. Then the sisters leave me alone with the microphone and the recorder. I rehearse my sermon by repeating it again into the mike, which helps me to focus my attention and stimulates my mental faculties. The sisters are back at 6:15, and they push me in the wheelchair to the elevator. We descend from the roof-deck to the ground floor, and then begin the slow journey of about 500 meters to the gymnasium where about 4,000 youngsters have been assembled and are sitting quietly on the floor waiting for Mass to begin. Offering Mass and speaking to the children used to be a consolation, but in the words of the *Imitation of Christ*, "The Lord now has turned into dust all the consolations of the earth." Mass, which used to be consoling, is simply another painful experience and entails a struggle. My pronunciation is very slurred and my voice is so weak, I have to speak with my lips almost kissing the mike. Although I try to speak as slowly and distinctly as possible, at times my voice cracks and breaks.

Occasionally during Mass, flies get into the act and add to the excitement. They play games by landing on my nose, then my forehead, and occasionally my ears or the back of my hands. I wonder if Jesus had a similar form of torture on Calvary. None of the gospel writers speak of the role of the flies in the Passion of Christ. But it was hot, it was the middle of the afternoon and there were a lot of people milling about drinking and probably eating. So I imagine there were many flies around also and that some of them added to the torment of the Savior.

The children are a model congregation. They are self-disciplined, fervent and attentive. When I speak to them they are quiet and seem to hang on my every word. They pray with enthusiasm and their singing is enthusiastic and alive. The rondalla band acts as a marvelous back-up to the children and adds much joy and verve to the liturgy.

After Mass the sisters get me to my feet and remove the vestments. With the sisters supporting me on each side, I stand for a few minutes trying to cool off because I am now sweating profusely. Since the onset of ALS, I have become extremely sensitive to cold and heat. As with so many other things in this deteriorating body of mine, the temperature-regulating system also is mal-functioning. I drink some ice water, and after cooling off a bit, I am put back into my wheelchair.

The sisters wheel me back to my room and place me on an exercise bike. They strap my hands with velcro tape so that I do not fall off. Then I slowly start pushing the pedals and do my version of a work-out for 15 or 20 minutes.

Before, when one was diagnosed with ALS, the experts advised him to crawl into bed and stay there. They thought the best way to survive this strange and rare illness was to remain inactive and to conserve one's remaining strength and energy. But, as is so often the case, the so-called-medical experts have now come full circle and advise the very opposite.

I'm not sure my ultimate goal is to survive as long as possible. But since I have been very active physically all my life, I try to continue to do what I can. I am very grateful that I can still sit on a bike and move the pedals on my own power.

After my session on the bike, sister brings me a balloon. In order to strengthen my rapidly-deteriorating-breathing muscles, I practice blowing up a balloon a couple times a day. Blowing a balloon sounds like a very innocuous activity, but really it has an element of risk and excitement. On a number of occasions I have had balloons blow up in my face and in the face of the sister assisting me. This is always a surprise and causes both of us to burst into laughter. Frequently the sister holding the balloon moves her face away from it in anticipation of another explosion. She becomes nervous and a little giggly. This in turn affects me and in order to blow up the balloon I have to control my giddiness and my nervousness. This morning, no balloons blew up in my face.

Next with a sister supporting me on each side, I do some more exercises. I sway back and forth, up and down, and side to side. Then after sitting me in my wheelchair, the sisters put me through some range-of-motion exercises. They move my arms, hands, wrists, fingers and so on. This therapy is helpful in keeping my joints from freezing or solidifying.

Following therapy, I sit at the table, listening to some classical music as one of the sisters begins to feed me breakfast. My swallowing muscles are now affected by the disease. I gag and choke easily, so I eat very small bites, chew slowly, and swallow very carefully. Eating is now more pain than pleasure. I do it more out of a sense of duty than from appetite or desire.

After breakfast, the sisters get me ready again for the 9:00 o'clock Mass for our TB out-patients at Quezon Institute In Manila. About 1,500 strong, they have already assembled and are waiting for me in the gym where I say Mass. I put my sermon for the TB patients on a tape the day before and gave it to Brother Tony. He has transcribed and translated it into Tagalog. As I read the English version, Brother Tony translates it into Tagalog. Brother's voice is clear, sharp and enthusiastic. His presence on the altar is strong and spiritual. One day, with God's grace, after ordination, I think Brother Tony will make an outstanding preacher and teacher of the word of God.

After the Mass for the TB patients, I am brought back to my room where I have scheduled a meeting with Sister Michaela and Sister Tess. Among other issues, we discuss plans for the inauguration of our new Boystown facilities at Silang in the Philippines scheduled for July 23, 1991 which will be presided over by Cardinal Sin. We also discuss Sister Michaela's and Sister Risa's trip to the Bicol region. The two of them plan to leave on the afternoon plane for Legaspi. Their purpose is to round up, interview and select another 200 children who are needy, hungry and out of school to fill up the current vacancies at our Boystown and Girlstown. The sisters assure me there will be no problem in filling the quota. The problem will be limiting the number of those who would like to be included on our list.

After concluding the meeting with the sisters, I go over some printed material which arrived yesterday by overnight mail from my fund-raising office in Maryland. I look over the appeal letters, the photographs and contribution cards which I myself prepared and sent to Maryland about ten days ago. I note in my mind a few modifications and corrections, although in general, the material looks acceptable.

Before lunch, I go through my routine again on the stationary bicycle, the balloon blowing, the standing exercises, and the range-of-motion exercises. This is followed by some massage therapy, which the sisters administer. This entire routine fills up

41

an hour or so. This is followed by lunch consisting of a cheese sandwich on whole wheat bread, washed down by a glass of Tang, plus a banana or apple. Afterwards, I lie in bed resting for about 30 minutes or so. Later in the afternoon, I get in a car with the sisters, and we head for our Boystown in Silang, Cavite. We usually recite the rosary together on our way to the Boystown.

We arrive at Silang about four in the afternoon. Sister Teresita smiling and radiating joyful energy is waiting at the kitchen door with my wheelchair. Before Mass, which is scheduled to begin at five, I hear confessions of some of the older boys.

After Mass, I have supper at about 6:00 o'clock. As I eat, I watch the evening news on the American, Far East or Philippines networks. Following supper, I prepare a recording of the meditation which I plan to give the sisters the next morning before Mass. Then sister wheels me to the roof-deck chapel where I try to spend an hour or so in prayer.

I call my evening prayer a round-the-clock meditation because my head is weaving, bobbing and swaying as I try to fight off fatigue and sleep. After my evening prayers, I watch television for an hour or so. Most of the programs are pretty inane and insipid, but to date I have not been able to come up with a better way of getting through an hour or two before it is time to go to bed. At times I listen to recordings of spiritual books, or the gospels, but frequently I find that I am dozing as the reader drones on.

About 9:00 o'clock, I call the sisters on the speaker system which joins our two rooms. We go through more range of motion exercises and a massage therapy routine, similar to what I did at noon. Then they try to make me as comfortable as possible in bed. This is not easy because of the ALS, the severe arthritis in my right hip and shoulder and to a lesser extent the arthritis on my left side as well. It gets uncomfortable and the pain often wakes me up. Since I am unable to move, I must call one of the sisters to assist me. It is not uncommon during the night to summon one of the sisters four or five times to assist me in one way or another. They change my position, get me a drink of water, put a blanket on me, close a window, or get me some medication and so on.

My Sunday routine and my daily routine changes from week to week depending on where I am geographically (i.e.

Korea, the Philippines or Mexico) or where I am physically in the state of my disease. Describing a more or less typical day reminds me of the title of the play by Eugene O'Neill called *A Long Days Journey Into Night*. The days tend to be tedious and it is a challenge to make it through to the night.

On the other hand, with increasing problems with sleep and further physical deterioration the night presents its own challenges. In the psalms I have read frequently the expression, "the terror of the nights." Until now it had little meaning for me, but now I look at the night with a sense of terror. I look at my bed as, more or less, an enemy. It is a challenge to make it through to the dawn. There is a French song composed by a Jesuit priest which goes like this, "Pourquoi, pourquoi Seigneur fais-tu la nuit si longue pour moi? Toi qui fais de si belles choses, pourquoi, fais-tu la nuit si longue?" A rough translation is, "Why, oh why, my God, have You made the night so long, so long for me? You have made such beautiful things, but why have You made the night so long?"

Chapter 6

My Unfinished Symphony

U pon my return to Korea, a great inner struggle began. The struggle was not directly related to my illness. Rather, the struggle was centered on the discernment of the will of the Lord. Was it truly the will of the Lord — or just my personal whim — that I go to Mexico and begin our Boystown and Girlstown programs in that country?

This I think was the most difficult decision of my life. Most of the decisions I make are in the 60 to 40 percent range. That is, the reasons for making the decision outweigh those which negate the decision are usually about 60 percent to 40 percent. The Mexico decision, however, was more in the 51 percent to 49 percent range. It was an extremely close and difficult call. There were perhaps about 15 or more reasons on the pro side of the decision. If any one, or at least two, of these reasons were eliminated the decision would have swayed to the con side of the argument and the Sisters of Mary would not be in Mexico today as I write these lines.

I have no set formula for discerning the will of the Lord in my life. I try my best simply to follow the example of Jesus in the Garden of Gethsemane as He agonized over the decision to accept or reject his coming passion and death.

Jesus entered the darkness of the garden. He was prostrate on the ground with his face pressed to the earth. The inner anguish, struggle and turmoil was so great that he sweated blood. So many reasons for not going ahead with his passion came to mind. First of all, he asked Himself the question, "Is this horrible suffering, terrible pain, most repulsive humiliation and demeaning death necessary?" If I have to die, surely there must be an easier, more comfortable and more dignified way. For example, John the Baptist suffered death by having his head quickly and quietly severed from his body. Also, consider this, the majority of men are really not interested in salvation, so will not all this blood, sweat and tears be a waste? Moreover, what sin or evil have I done to deserve such punishment and humiliation? Most of these questions arose from the human nature of Jesus. Also, the devil was there to sharpen the questions and make them stronger.

Jesus continued His struggle. In the horrible night, He sought the light and it was given to Him by an angel of the Lord, who came to comfort Him. The angel put the light of God in His heart and the strength of God in His soul. Jesus rose from His agony, His heart was now calm, serene and at peace, in the knowledge of what the Father desired of Him. However, the struggle continued to the very end, the doubts continued to assail His mind and soul. On Calvary He is still in the darkness crying out almost in despair, "My God, my God, why have you abandoned Me?" But deep underneath the surface struggle, hesitation and doubt, there was this quiet light and strong peace which never left Jesus.

The agony of Jesus lasted perhaps for an hour or so. The anguish, however, that I experienced in making this Mexico decision, went on for weeks and months. Moreover, even after the decision was made, I was continually assailed by lingering doubts and unanswered questions. As I write these lines now, however, about eighteen months after I arrived at the initial decision, I feel a deep inner peace that it was the Lord who inclined my heart towards Latin America and led me to Mexico.

After my return to Korea, I quickly made an appointment to visit one of the Mexican Missionaries of Guadalupe who had been working in Pusan for sometime. Way back in 1961, I was the one who initially wrote the Missionaries of Guadalupe in Mexico City inviting them to Pusan in the name of Bishop Choi. Also, in that same year, I went with Bishop Choi to Mexico City and helped with the negotiations and eventual decision to bring the Mexican Fathers to Korea and specifically to Pusan.

I visited one of the Mexican Fathers who was the young pastor of the parish they had built on the outskirts of Pusan. Mexicans have two or three family names and you're never sure which one is the real name to work with. Even now I am not fully sure of the name of the priest I was talking to, so I will simply call him Father Sanchez. I outlined to Father Sanchez what I had in mind. I emphasized, however, that if I wanted to launch our programs in Mexico City, there was no way that I could do it alone. Especially at this juncture in my life, I needed lots of help. I asked Father Sanchez if he would be willing to write his superior general in Mexico City and ask if he was willing to assist me in my Mexican venture? Father Sanchez was most cordial and encouraging and was happy to write his superior general. A reply was received very quickly stating that the superior general and his people would do their very best to assist me in any way possible. So, come to Mexico without delay!

About this time, I also wrote to Father Wason, an American priest I knew by name who was engaged in child welfare work near Mexico City for 35 years or so. Over the years, I had exchanged mailing lists with Father Wason, but we had never had any direct contact or even correspondence until now. I wrote Father Wason asking for his advice and suggestions. He answered quickly with a reply which was most encouraging and positive. He also urged me to come to Mexico City and promised he would do all in his power to assist me.

As always, it has been my habit to discuss every decision I make with the sisters, from the youngest to the oldest, to get their input and feedback. The sisters are a courageous, zealous, apostolic group. They listened to my Mexican project with open minds and courageous hearts and reacted with dynamic enthusiasm. Their only reservation was with my health. But outside of that, in essence, they said, "Wherever you go, Father, we will follow." If I ever had the misfortune to lead them off a cliff and plunge into the sea, they would merrily and happily follow me.

From a strictly rational and human point of view, to go to Mexico at this juncture in my life seemed like the height of folly. First of all, I had a terminal illness. My days were not only numbered but the days in which I would be functional were even more strictly numbered.

Also, our work in the Philippines was expanding. We were building in Cebu and purchasing land outside Manila, in Silang, Cavite, for further construction. What is more, we had invitations from a number of bishops throughout the Philippines to set up our Boystown and Girlstown programs in their dioceses. The opportunities were unlimited. Moreover, we were quite familiar with the culture, the climate, the language and the problems in the Philippines. It would be infinitely easier if we were determined to grow and expand, to do it within the Philippines than half a world away, in another climate and culture such as to be found in Mexico.

Moreover, there was the question of finances to be considered. Mexico would be expensive, certainly not as expensive as Korea but much more expensive than the Philippines. My finances were very limited and my present commitments were already enormous. Instead of thinking of expanding and consuming more money, I should be thinking of putting money in the bank to establish an endowment fund for the future security and stability of programs already begun. I was juggling all these ideas in my mind, weighing the pros and the cons, praying a great deal, getting advice from many people and at the same time, watching with one eye as my physical condition continued to deteriorate and each day I could see myself getting a little weaker. I was very much like "a child in the night, a child crying for the light, with no other voice but a cry."

During the week of January 15, I gave the annual retreat of the sisters which was followed by the annual renewal of vows. In my heart, before advancing to the altar to celebrate the Mass during which vows were to be solemnly renewed, I made a special intention for that particular Mass. The intention of course centered on the Mexican decision. I was not seeking a spectacular thunderbolt or flash of lightning but I wanted some indication, just a little inner movement or inclination of the heart concerning what the Lord wanted me to do with regards to Mexico.

That particular Mass was a memorable one. I became quite ill while vesting before Mass but decided to go ahead with the liturgy which was a mistake. After advancing to the altar and kissing it, I blessed myself and started to recite the prayers at the beginning of Mass. To my horror and humiliation, I discovered that I had no voice. I struggled mightily but I could hardly make myself heard and what came out was hardly comprehensible. I was convinced that it was ALS doing its thing. Later on, however, I changed my judgment of this strange phenomenon and attributed it to some passing weakness and sickness.

As I recall, that particular Mass was characterized by a good deal of sobbing and a lot of tears on the part of the sisters. I spotted a priest who happened to be standing in the back of the chapel. I invited him to vest and take my place at the altar which he most graciously did.

I was greatly discomforted by this turn of events. At the same time, however, they brought a certain secret peace to my heart. I felt that this was the answer of the Lord and it was a resounding rejection of this wild Mexican venture. I felt a certain disappointment but at the same time I inwardly breathed a great sigh of relief.

After Mass, I made my way to my room. I worked out a bit on my exercise bike, took a hot shower, had a small lunch, then rested for a while. The sisters paid me a visit and we discussed the weird event which took place at the beginning of Mass. I said, certainly this must be an indication from the Lord that the Mexican venture should be put on hold. The sisters, God bless them, took the opposite side of the argument. They countered, "How do you know, Father, that this was not simply a tactic of the devil to mislead you?" I wanted them to reassure me and help me to abandon the Mexican venture. Here they were, however, sowing more doubt and taking the opposite tack. The heart of the matter was I really did not know for sure, one way or another, what the Lord wanted.

About this time, I received an invitation from Archbishop Dias, the Apostolic Nuncio and very good friend and long-time confidant of mine to dine with him at the Nunciature. I spoke to him about the Mexican project and sought his advice. Being of clear mind and sound judgment, I felt that he would certainly advise against it. Once again, I was totally mistaken.

He urged me, very strongly and enthusiastically, to go ahead with the project. He said, "You begin it but you do not have to finish it. Others will do that. This will be your unfinished symphony."

These were nice words. However, it has never been my style to write, conduct or launch unfinished symphonies. I feel compelled to finish whatever I begin. However, the words of the Nuncio struck deep and they always filled my consciousness when doubts and fears assailed me. I would say to myself. "Do not be so proud and think you are the only one who can do anything. You begin it, others will finish it. This will be your great and glorious unfinished symphony." Deep down inside, however, try as I would, I could not find these words totally convincing. I admired the Nuncio and respected him greatly but I secretly wondered, does he have any idea what is involved here? We are not talking about opening a little day-care center or a bookstore. We are talking about beginning a Boystown or Girlstown which eventually will accommodate five to ten thousand needy and underprivileged children.

The problems to be solved are enormous. The project is vast in scope. The difficulties to be encountered will certainly be overwhelming. I have little money, few people to assist me, no one on my team who has any knowledge of Spanish. To get started in Mexico City, I will need to find a large piece of land, get permission from government and Church authorities, set up non-profit corporations, open bank accounts, contact builders we can trust, and recruit Mexican candidates willing to join and work with the sisters. Also and perhaps most importantly, the total concept of our Boystown and Girlstown is very new, original and unorthodox. Would the parents of poor children buy the idea, in a word, would it work in Mexico? Deep inside I felt that the Apostolic Nuncio did not have full understanding of what was involved here. However, I always thought of and spoke of this venture as my "unfinished symphony."

After the annual retreat and renewal of vows in Korea, I flew to the Philippines. Shortly after my arrival, I was invested with the so-called dignity of monsignorship or honorary prelateship or whatever other "ship" you call this sort of ceremony. However, I will save this for another chapter and serve it up as a little comic interlude.

After a month or so in the Philippines, I returned to Korea. It was now around the end of February. At the urging of the sisters,

I decided to invite a few priest-friends for lunch to celebrate my investiture as an honorary prelate. I gave the names of a few close priest-friends to the sisters and asked them to phone and invite these and only these. I purposely omitted the names of the Mexican Fathers in Pusan. In my heart of hearts, I had now written off the Mexican venture as pure folly. I did not want to see any priests from Mexico for fear that they might shake me from my new-found serenity in the rejection of the Mexican project.

I entered the dining room where the priests had gathered for lunch to greet them and exchange some jokes. To my stupefaction, I saw one of the Mexican Fathers. As happens frequently at my place, there was miscommunication and indirectly one of the sisters had invited him to attend. We immediately started talking about my Mexican plans. He said that his superior general and their people were expecting to see me around the beginning of March. I did speak of a possible trip at that time and this was a possible date but nothing had been decided, yet "They were expecting me." These words hit me over the head like a hammer and shook me up.

It is not my nature to promise something and then renege. I hate to break a promise or not to honor my word no matter what. I did ask for help. They said they would give it. I did say I was coming on a certain date and they were expecting me. I felt pushed and inwardly bullied but I hesitated.

From Korea I called Father Wason who was in Arizona at that time. I discussed with him my doubts concerning the Mexican project. He did his best to allay them. He encouraged me forcefully to come without delay. I hung up the phone shaking my head with wonderment. Somehow, it all seemed like a tender trap and I felt myself slowly but surely being caught.

I felt like Juan Diego to whom Our Lady of Guadalupe first appeared in 1531. Because of a commitment to a sick uncle, Juan Diego also tried to avoid Our Lady of Guadalupe by taking another path below the hill where she was always waiting for him. But lo and behold, as he was tiptoeing along this other route, he looked up and there she was, smilingly blocking the way and waiting for him. Now this was my experience. It seemed as if I were desperately trying to avoid this beautiful and mysterious

Virgin of Guadalupe. I would go this way and that way, try this and that excuse but she was always there, waiting for me, blocking my path and gently leading me in the direction of Mexico. At times I would look at her portrait and sometimes think of her as a loving opponent. No matter what I tried she was always there and eventually, of course, she had her way and did get me to Mexico.

There I was in Korea, wavering, hesitating and agonizing. However, on Saturday, I called from Pusan to talk to my assistant in Seoul, Damiano Park. I instructed Damiano to make reservations on a flight for Mexico via Los Angeles on Tuesday. I would decide on Monday whether or not to go. On Monday, I decided to give it a try — if for no other reason than to make a pilgrimage to the Shrine of Guadalupe and pay my respects to this very beautiful and persistent Lady.

I left for Mexico sometime on Monday. As the plane was descending over Mexico City, I heard the pilot announce my name on the loudspeaker. He said that someone would be waiting for me at the terminal. Sure enough, Father Wason and an airport official were waiting for me. They escorted me through customs as if I were a visiting dignitary or head of state.

Father Wason drove me in his car to the central office of the Missionaries of Guadalupe where I stayed for one week. The Guadalupe Fathers were extremely kind and helpful. They had assigned one priest whom I shall call Father Antonio, to be my guide and assistant during my stay in Mexico City.

My first stop with Father Antonio was to the Shrine of Our Lady of Guadalupe. I first visited this world-popular Marian Shrine in 1961 in the company of Bishop Choi. I visited it a second time in 1968 when I came to Mexico City with the thought of setting up an international mission society. Here I was again in 1990 at this beautiful shrine which was always filled with humble, devout, mostly family people. After my visit to the shrine, we took a tour of some of the slums on the outskirts of Mexico City, especially those in the Neza area and later Chalco.

Although my stay in Mexico City was brief, I came away with a strong impression that the culture of Mexico and the problems of the country and the Church were remarkably similar to those of the Philippines. There was indeed great poverty in

Mexico. Although statistically the country was perhaps more than twice as prosperous as the Philippines, the poor in Mexico looked poorer than in the Philippines. For one thing, in Mexico, the slum-dwellers had to contend with the bitter cold, the rain, the mud and terrible transportation problems. Also, the level of education in Mexico was much lower than in the Philippines.

Mexico City is the largest city in the world, with an estimated population of 20 million people. It is also estimated that the city increases by a thousand people a day — people streaming in from the provinces and the country sides in search of jobs and a better way of life.

As in the Philippines, the Church in Mexico was being decimated. Especially, the Church was losing many of the poor, uneducated and the lowly — the very ones who have priority in the work of salvation. Born-agains, Fundamentalists, Jehovah's Witnesses, Mormons and many similar sects were sending their missionaries to Mexico with suitcases full of money in an effort to buy away souls.

Frequently, it works something like this. A Born-again or a Fundamentalist will contact a Catholic catechist who has been working for the Church for many years with little or no remuneration. How much are you being paid, they ask? The catechist shrugs his shoulders and answers, nothing really. We will give you so much, and usually it is a generous sum to come and work for us. The temptation is very strong to apostatize. In addition to this, frequently there is a premium or a bounty for each warm-blooded convert brought into the ranks of the invading sects (i.e. so many pesos given per convert or per soul). Moreover, many of these religious marauders are enthusiastic faith-healers and charismatics. There are few medical services available to the poor so they are greatly attracted to any type of free healing, even if it is faith-healing or charismatic ministry. Also, the animated "Amen, Praise the Lord! Alleluia," shouting and stamping, hooting and hollering, emotional and animated style of the newcomers appeals greatly to the poor slum-dwellers. Also, there are many scandals frequently involving money, power and corruption in the Church in Mexico which help further to alienate people.

But of all the reasons which brought me to Mexico, the

strongest is the opportunity for apostolic work. Our Boystown and Girlstown programs are not just social welfare, humanitarian programs but they have a very strong and dynamic apostolic thrust. We take the children of the poor, children who are out-of-school, malnourished and who have no hope for the future.

These children are a marvelous to-date, untapped and undiscovered spiritual resource. Our goal is to turn them into lay apostles and to make them witnesses for the new, rejuvenated Church. These children will be the future elite for Christ and the Church and will help to stop the terrible spiritual hemorrhaging which is taking place in the Church in Mexico.

Although my stay in Mexico City was brief, it was very memorable. I had an interview with the Bishop of the Neza–Chalco area. He was most enthusiastic when he learned of my programs and projects. He too urged me to come. He promised full support and the support of all his clergy.

The Guadalupe Fathers also urged me to make a positive decision. I talked with one of their priests who had twice been elected superior general. He urged me to come. He said, "Father, remember, still waters become stagnant and polluted; whereas, running waters always remain fresh, clear and vibrant." In other words, he was telling me, do not stay timidly locked up in just Korea and the Philippines. Be bold, break out and expand. I thought of the words of Cardinal Newman, "Therein lies the nobility of faith to have the courage to dare something." I did not believe I lacked courage. Rather I feared I had a lack of wisdom or even common sense. "Prudence is better than valor," it is written in Scripture. The question still unresolved in my mind was, what was the will of the Lord.

However, I had an experience as a young boy of ten on a high diving-board. It was reputed to be one of the highest in the city of Washington. It was a matter of honor to have taken the plunge. I knew the one way to do it was to climb right up to the edge and dive in without hesitating. If I hesitated, looked down, looked back, looked up and looked around, I would never make the dive. I felt if I ever hoped to get something started in Mexico City, I could not leave without making a decision and planting the seed.

Father Antonio liked what he heard concerning my programs and projects. He offered his services and said he would be more than willing to help me and even work for me if it was okay with his superior. So before I left, I effectively pushed the button and the light turned green. I told Father Antonio to look for land and suitable contractors and to look into the laws applicable to establishing non-profit corporations, opening up of bank accounts and so on, so that we could set up a Mexican foundation. I paid a final, quick visit to Our Lady of Guadalupe. I thanked her for bringing me there and I prayed that if it pleased the Lord, she would bring me back again, this time with the sisters, to set up the foundation. I left Mexico and flew back to Korea. On the way back, I felt peace but at the same time, there was lingering doubt and a nagging concern that I was making a mistake, perhaps the biggest mistake in my life.

But it had begun. The first notes of my unfinished symphony were floating in the air and for better or worse, we, or at least I, was off and running.

Chapter 7

The Technicolor Priest

The fifth chapter was entitled "Long Day's Journey." The title turned out to be very fitting because the chapter turned out to be very long. To make up for chapter five, I will try to make this chapter very short.

The definition of a monsignor is a priest in technicolor. I was invested with the title of Honorary Prelate or Domestic Prelate or Right Reverend Monsignor, or whatever, on February 1, 1990. So now, I am a true-blue, super-duper priest in technicolor.

I thought it was something that would never happen to me. I was never a favorite with the hierarchy in Korea where I had spent most of my priestly life. The members of the hierarchy have the authority to invest one with this honor. So I was serene in the knowledge that there was little danger of this happening to me.

A friend of mine who was very acquainted with my confrontational relationship with the Korean Bishops compared me to Martin Luther, always with my wagons in a circle — Al Schwartz against the world. My being made monsignor can be compared to the Indians stopping their attack on the pioneers who have been encircled and endangered and under attack for many years. They call out the leader of the people in the wagons and announce that they have decided to make him an honorary Indian Chief. It can never be said that the holy Roman Catholic Church, for all its faults and weaknesses, ever lacked a sense of humor. Proof of this marvelous divinely-inspired, centuries-old sense of humor can be found in my investiture as an honorary prelate.

Until 1969, I was the fair-haired boy of the Bishop of Pusan. After that, I became the outcast, not only of the Bishop of Pusan but because most of the bishops in Korea are very close, the outcast of Korea. What dastardly deed did I do in 1969 to become the outcast of the Korean hierarchy? In 1969, I stopped giving money to my bishop because I was convinced he was misusing it. The money was designated for the poor and I felt it was not being used for this sacred purpose. I could write a book of what transpired but the heart of the matter is as simple as writing a check. I announced that I was no longer willing to write and give checks to my bishop or any of the other bishops of Korea. After months, even years, of negotiations and efforts to persuade and compromise my decision, my bishop let out a kind of primal scream that could be heard as far as North Korea. He literally struck the table and I felt that he was very close to striking me.

After that, he and his successors, on various occasions and at various times tried; one, to have me thrown out of the diocese; two, to have me deported from Korea; three, to have me suspended as a priest; four, to sabotage my efforts to raise funds overseas for the poor; and five, to close down and destroy the Sisters of Mary, the Boystown and Girlstown, and all my other works of charity. The fact that their desires were thwarted is a tribute to the grace and mercy of God.

Also, with one major exception, I was never very popular with the Apostolic Nuncios who came to Korea. I have had dealings with six or seven of them. I remember vividly in the height of my battle for survival with the Bishop of Pusan the Apostolic Nuncio called me in. He advised me with great seriousness that I should leave the priesthood and the Church. I pointed out that this was strong advice and I innocently asked what was the basis of this advice. His reply was a very eloquent shrug of the shoulders and he threw his hands up in the Italian gesture which says no explanation is really necessary. The fact of the matter was I was making waves in the diocese of Pusan and rocking the boat. He was getting a little seasick and so he thought the way to solve the matter was to throw me overboard just as this seemed to be the answer for Jonas in days of old.

However, six months to a year later, my fortunes changed

and my star was now ascending. The same Apostolic Nuncio came to Pusan, phoned me one Sunday morning and asked if he could come to say Mass for the sisters and have lunch with me. I immediately accepted and at lunch we spoke as if we were lifelong buddies. I was being educated in church politics.

As I mentioned before, Cardinal Sin came to Korea for the International Eucharistic Congress. After saying Mass at my Boystown, we had breakfast together. At breakfast, he made the astounding announcement that he had discussed the matter with the other bishops in the Philippines and they all agreed that some recognition should be given to the work I was doing there. So it was decided that they would make me a Monsignor, not just a Monsignor, but one of the highest ranks, namely, an Honorary Prelate. This bit of news caught me by surprise. I only smiled. The Cardinal did not ask whether I wanted to be made Monsignor or not. He simply advised me of his decision to go ahead with the matter. He went on to say he had discussed the matter with the apostolic delegate in Manila. He agreed to recommend me to Rome with the proviso that my Bishop in Pusan give his consent. Again, I said nothing, but in my mind I laughed. I was convinced that my Bishop, if he were in possession of his right mind, would never consent to this. It would only make him look like a fool in the eyes of his fellow Bishops. Also, it was very rare, in fact, I've never heard of a priest being invested with the honor of Monsignorship in a diocese and by a Bishop other than his own. The whole thing was a bit ludicrous and bizarre.

As soon as Cardinal Sin saw my Bishop at the blessing of our new Girlstown building in Pusan, he drew him aside and they were engaged for some time in intense discussion. I glanced at the two now and then and I was convinced that my Bishop would refuse Cardinal Sin's request. When we got back to Seoul, Cardinal Sin happily told me my Bishop was a very nice man and that he had given his consent.

Still in my heart, I did not think the matter would go through. I thought some document would come to my Bishop for signature and he would put it in a drawer and forget about it, or the documents would go to Rome and sit there until they grew moldy. However, I underestimated the prowess of Cardinal Sin. The matter went right through and within a few weeks, impressive documents signed by Pope John Paul II himself investing me with the title of Honorary Prelate were delivered to the Cardinal in Manila. I was tempted to write the Cardinal and decline the honor. I lived very happily as a simple priest and I would be happy to die as such. I did not like to be called Monsignor and I wanted to keep the title of "Father." I hesitated to write because I thought the matter would not go through, and secondly, I did not want to unnecessarily offend Cardinal Sin.

By telephone between Manila and Korea, I requested that the investiture ceremony take place at my Boystown/Girlstown in Manila. I thought it would be good for the morale of the children and the sisters. Also, I selected the date of February 1 which was a day when I could be in Manila after completing the annual sisters' retreat and the graduations at the end of January.

The Cardinal sent his personal tailor to fit me with the necessary robes. I was shocked when I saw them because they were not just red but scarlet. They had a million buttons and a huge cincture with a lot of tassels. When I tried them on I did not know whether I looked like somebody's mother or a clown. Probably, I looked a little of both.

I was very nervous for many days before the ceremony. My health was rapidly deteriorating. I was afraid my legs might collapse under me during the ceremony and I was also worried that my voice might not be functional. However, as it turned out, all these fears proved groundless.

The ceremony was set for 8 o'clock in the morning, and it turned out to be something grand and glorious and surprisingly very spiritual and moving. As I've said before, God gives us breathing space. He gives us this little taste of honey in preparation for the future bitter medicine. This was one of those breathing spaces or tastes of honey.

There were about twenty prelates in attendance including the Apostolic Delegate, Cardinal Vidal, Cardinal Sin and many Archbishops and Bishops. President Aquino was invited and sent her personal secretary with a letter and a gift and an invitation for me to visit her in the afternoon.

It was a beautiful day and the singing of the children during the Mass was extremely touching. The mass I chose for the day was the votive Mass of the Precious Blood. So even during Mass, red vestments were worn. I gave a little talk in which I mentioned that the priest, not just the Monsignor, was another Christ, and the color red was a reminder that as Christ He was also priest and victim. The priest was called to mingle his blood with that of Christ to redeem the world and, to borrow a phrase from St. Paul, "to make up in his own flesh the sufferings lacking to the body of Christ." As I stood on the platform during Mass with my red robes and later the red vestments, I felt very much like Jesus. And I thought of the Ecce Homo pictures where Jesus is covered with blood and He wore this as a red robe of blood and humiliation. Deep inside I had a foreboding that this was the future that awaited me. During Mass, I prayed for patience, courage and the determination to be faithful to Jesus until the end.

After Mass, there were happy picture-taking ceremonies with all the assembled Bishops and pictures with the sisters and the children. The mood was light and festive. In the afternoon, I went with a few sisters and we had a nice visit with President Aquino who is always kind, warm and charming.

After returning to Korea, everyone wanted to see me in my red Monsignor robes. I felt a little foolish but finally gave in and wore the robes for a wedding at which I officiated for my graduates. The second time I was going to wear the robes was for another wedding but to my surprise, the cincture slipped down to my knees. I had lost weight and did not have enough in my belly to support this cincture. So I gave up and never wore the robes again. Maybe I will be buried in the robes and I like that idea, because they are for me a symbol of the blood of Christ and a symbol of the vocation of sacerdos et victima, priest and victim.

Chapter 8

The Teachers' Strike

Our God is unpredictable. He is a God of surprises. The teachers' strike which began in April of 1990 and ended at the end of May the same year, was a surprise sent by God, and completely unexpected. I would classify the teachers' strike at our Boystown/Girlstown in Manila as one of the major crises in my life.

At first, I misjudged the situation and treated it in a rather cavalier manner. But as it turned out, it was deadly serious. It became apparent that the ultimate goal of the teachers was the takeover of our Boystown and Girlstown. Our goal was to remake each of the children entrusted to us into the image and likeness of Christ. The leaders of the striking teachers wanted to take over the education program in order to remake the children into their own image and likeness which was, to express it very charitably, very secular and very un-Christlike. St. Paul writes, "Whoever is the friend of the world is an enemy of God." The leaders of the striking teachers were very much friends of the modern world. To give but one example, they objected strongly to the clear, sharp, but balanced guidelines we laid down and gave our children concerning the virtue of chastity. Also, it must be said that some of the striking teachers had the reputation of being gay and the personal lives of some of them was far from exemplary.

Although the strike turned out to be a major crisis in which we were fighting for the very life of our institution, we came out of it stronger, wiser and purer than before. Just as gold and silver are purified by fire, so the heart of man is purified in the crucible of tribulation. The strike was a great purifying episode and a great learning experience for all of us.

To do justice to a description of the strike would require a full book rather than one brief chapter. However, my purpose now is to put in writing the major points and omit many of the details.

The seed of the strike was sown a year before when I decided to fire five trouble-making teachers. Before biting the bullet and letting them go, I gave them every opportunity to save their jobs. The Sister in charge of education met with them, our lawyer met with them, and I called them in one by one and tried to persuade them to change their ways. Their ways were, in general, liberal and to the left. They were always complaining, criticizing, and fomenting discord and discontent. There was never a problem regarding wages because our wages were exactly double that of what teachers in government schools were being paid. There was never a question concerning working conditions, because our facilities are first rate. In every way, we were extremely generous to our teachers. In return, we demanded hard work, enthusiasm and loyalty.

At first this group of five, although disruptive and dissatisfied, was manageable. Then they set up a meeting with a well known, liberal, human rights type of Bishop in the Manila Archdiocese. The Bishop did not so much as give us the courtesy of a phone call to get our side of the story. He admittedly sided with this group of five and sat down and wrote a strong letter to the Cardinal.

The good Cardinal was very supportive of our program but he hates confrontation and always wants to placate everyone. The Cardinal met with the group of five. In fact he wined and dined them. He also gave them the wrong impression that he was in their corner. In fact, he indirectly guaranteed them tenure at our school, no matter what happened. After their meeting with the Cardinal, a priest from the Cardinal's office paid me a visit, spoke about this group of five teachers and indirectly let it be known that it was the Cardinal's wish, that no matter what happened, they should not be terminated. I listened to what the priest had to say, and let most of it pass over my head, without even acknowledging exceptions or commenting on it in one way or another.

However, after this group of five met with the very liberal Bishop and the non-confrontational Cardinal, they became unmanageable. Each day was getting worse and they were influencing the other teachers. Despite the fact that they were in the middle of a year's contract and it was illegal, I decided to terminate them. Later, with our lawyer, we worked out a financial arrangement that was fair and just. I realized it would be expensive for us, but it seemed to be the only way to preserve our institution.

After the five left us, one or two of them continued to conspire on the outside with some of the teachers who remained on our staff. I was not aware of it at the time but one of this group of five was the ring leader behind the teachers' strike which erupted the following year.

As an interesting footnote, sometime later, when I was visiting with the Cardinal, he brought up the subject of these five teachers and indirectly implied that he was in error. After we let them go, one of this group turned on the Cardinal and wrote him several abusive letters concerning a matter completely unrelated to our problem. Afterwards, the Bishop paid us a visit and by his flattering manner and words, he indicated that he was not proud of how he had handled this matter.

The following year, in consultation with our lawyer, we prepared carefully worded one year contracts for each teacher in order to protect ourselves from a repeat performance by teachers like the group of five. The contracts were due to expire at the end of the school year in May. Those who would not be renewed were to be given one month's notice of our non-renewal decision. The Sister in charge of education, after a number of meetings with other sisters and after getting the input of the students decided not to renew the contracts of about ten teachers out of a total of more than a hundred. These ten teachers called the other teachers to a meeting under the pretense of a birthday party for one of their members. At this meeting, they lied to the other teachers and said that fifty or so teachers were to be terminated. They urged the teachers, in order to save their jobs, to join them in a strike. Our school would not be able to function. We would have no choice but to give in and reinstate them on their terms.

Later, some of the teachers who were misled into joining the strikers, said that they were also physically threatened and intimidated. If they did not join with the striking teachers, their families or their wives would be subject to violence. At first, I had difficulty in accepting this type of report as true. Later, as I became more familiar with the strike culture and tradition of the Philippines, I realized that violence, the threat of violence, deception, lies, and anything else is acceptable during a strike in order to achieve what is considered a noble goal or a worthy objective.

During Holy Week, the strike began at first slowly within the Boystown complex. I got word by phone but Sister gave me no detailed report and she passed over the matter as something minor and unimportant. However, on the Tuesday after Easter, I was on the phone to Manila the whole day and after a number of probing, questioning phone calls, I concluded that the matter indeed was very serious. I also concluded that I should go to Manila at once.

That Tuesday was a memorable day. At breakfast, I reached for the newspaper and suddenly fell from my chair. This, of course, was due to the ALS disease. I hit the cement terrazo hard with the side of my cheek. I was more stunned than hurt. I put my fingers to my cheek and looked at them and was surprised to see that they were red with blood. Under my eye, I had a big fat red cherry about the size of a silver dollar. As I looked at myself in the mirror with surprise and amusement, somewhere in the depths of my heart, I heard a voice saying that this was a warning of the great trial and crisis which lay ahead.

This type of thing happened once before in my life. It was very prophetic and accurate. During the final year or so of my seminary training in Louvain, a new Superior General had been announced. The seminary and the society which ran it was in a state of complete disarray at that time. I heard the announcement at supper. Afterwards, in an expression of exhilaration, I was running around the refectory with another seminarian and we were laughing and throwing water on each other. The linoleum floor became wet and as I took a quick turn, I slipped suddenly, cracked the side of my cheek on the edge of a chair before I went down. I had a very bad bruise and swelling and a sore cheek for some time after that. It dawned on me that this was a warning of more blows which were to come with the new administration. This turned out to be very true. Now here, an almost identical warning to prepare spiritually and mentally was given to me again.

I was inwardly torn and distressed that Tuesday. That evening my three sisters (Schwartz's) with their spouses and some other friends were due to arrive in Seoul. They had been saving up for some time and this would be their first visit ever to me in the missions. I know it meant a great deal to them and also I was elated that they were finally coming to see me. The plans were for them to spend three or four days in Korea with me and then together, we would leave for the Philippines where they would spend another three or four days before departing for the U.S.

However, my first duty was to my children. So I had no choice but to leave them in the care of Damiano, my assistant in Korea, and to leave for the Philippines. I met them that night at the airport. It was a happy get together although their eyes grew wide when they saw the big red mark on the side of my cheek. We went together to their hotel and gathered around the table. I announced that I had to leave them in the morning and go to the Philippines. They were certainly pained by this announcement but I felt that they understood and supported my decision.

The next day I flew to Manila. Several of the Sisters met me at the airport. On the way to the Boystown, they briefed me on the state of emergency brought about by the teachers. As we approached our Boystown entrance, I was shocked by what I saw. Tents were pitched on both sides of the entrance where the teachers were sleeping at night. They were marching up and down with signs and placards denouncing the Sisters as tyrannical, dictatorial fascists. Also, they were physically blockading the entrance and controlling and dictating who could enter and who could leave.

Before entering the compound, I descended from the vehicle and a group of teachers immediately surrounded me. Naively, they thought that I would side with them and support their position. However, I let them know immediately that the opposite was true. I said that there was no way we would give in and there was no way we could take them back after such an act of betrayal and disloyalty. As it turned out, not one of the striking teachers, the number was about sixty, was ever reinstated.

The next morning, I said Mass in the gym for the children. At Mass, I spoke about obedience and loyalty. As events turned out, this choice of subject was inspired.

After Mass, I walked to the entrance of the compound to assess the situation. Really, we were under siege, blockaded, almost reduced to hostages or prisoners in our own house. All of this of course was illegal. But in the Philippines, during a strike, anything goes. Those in authority are afraid to interfere or meddle for fear that they will be the target of violence. Also, it should be pointed out, that violence is very much a part of the strike culture in the Philippines. When our strike finally ended about eight weeks later, the teachers were quite proud of the fact that there were no deaths. The teachers let me through their picket line and I walked down the road where some of our loyal teachers were waiting. They were not permitted to enter the Boystown/Girlstown even though they wanted to. The striking teachers thought they would bring us to our knees and with four thousand children and a handful of Sisters, chaos would reign without the teachers. However, we conducted business as usual. The Sisters arranged for the older students to teach the younger ones. They themselves helped with the teaching chores. They organized a very busy and active day and the striking teachers on the outside were astounded and dismayed to hear the happy sounds of a normally functioning Boystown and Girlstown coming from the other side of the wall.

As I was walking back towards the entrance to our compound, one or two of the striking teachers approached me. One held a microphone to my mouth and was asking questions and recording my answers. He was greatly agitated and frightened and shaking. The girls on the upper fifth and sixth floors of our Girlstown building were watching intently from a distance. Somehow, it seemed to the girls that the teacher had me by the throat and was manhandling me. Word went out that the striking teachers were beating up on Father. The girls became hysterical. They came pouring out of the building like it was on fire and headed for the striking teachers at the gate with fire in their eyes and hysterical looks on their faces. The boys immediately heard the rumor and they grabbed whatever broom, dustpan or chair that was nearby and could serve as a weapon and they too immediately headed for the action like a group of commandos storming the enemy. I was about fifty feet from the gate and did not realize what was happening. The girls and the boys were totally out of control. The Sisters tried to prevent them from going out but they went through the extended arms of the Sisters and headed for the teachers. The girls grabbed the female teachers and the boys came diving off the walls and onto the male teachers. The chaos lasted for less than two minutes and it was full of scenes and episodes that were hysterically funny. No one was really hurt although one newspaper carried headlines reporting that the students of the Sisters of Mary had mauled striking teachers. They manhandled the teachers and shook them up considerably but they did not maul anybody nor, happily, seriously injure anybody.

As soon as I realized what was happening, I ran to the children and shouted, "No, no, not this way." I made eye contact with the leaders of the children and after a moment's hesitation, they accepted what I told them and turned around and went inside. I had no problem with shaking up the teachers a bit but we must not go about it in this manner. It should be planned and organized and not so chaotic. Also, with the volatile Filipino character, this type of thing was filled with danger of serious bodily harm and violence which I wanted to avoid, if at all possible. This little episode shook the striking teachers to their roots. At first, certain that the children would side with them, now, they were utterly astounded to learn where their real loyalty lay.

I decided to send all the children home for several weeks of vacation. I wanted a cooling off period during which, we could negotiate with the striking teachers and settle the matter peacefully, perhaps with a monetary solution.

I prepared the children for their home visit by celebrating Mass and giving them a sermon. I told them their visit home was not a vacation but a home apostolate. They were to do three things, similar to what Jesus did to begin his public ministry. One, pray; two, teach the children catechism and religion; and three, help and serve the poor and needy. When the children came back, we interviewed them and were gratified to learn how fruitful and productive their home apostolate turned out to be.

Each day, the teachers became more desperate and they resorted to more and more drastic tactics. They also engaged the services of professional strikers and goons. I would see them sitting out there in the hot sun and this frightened me. One or two looked like they would stick up anybody for a pack of cigarettes or a bottle of beer. A couple of our teachers looked like they were on drugs. However, I have to give them credit, because even though it was frightfully hot, they camped out under their tents day and night for almost eight weeks.

They seriously misjudged the Sisters and underestimated our reaction. They thought we would become terrified at the thought of our reputations being soiled by teachers walking up and down with placards denouncing us. I had no problem what-soever with that. They were free to call us every name in the book and to denounce us to their hearts' content. I was greatly dis-turbed, however, by their illegal tactics, the physical blockade of the compound and the threat of physical violence. The Sisters, however, managed to keep our compound supplied with food and fuel by using every means imaginable. They brought supplies up the Pasig River by boat until the captains of the boats refused to do so because the teachers or their goons resorted to throwing rocks at them. Somehow the Sisters got the Philippine Coast Guard to escort the boats up the Pasig River. Also, we put in another entrance in the back of the compound. The teachers very quickly got wind of that but this dispersed their forces because it was another area which they had to guard. Also, the Sisters would come tearing down the road with their car and the Sisters on the other side of the fence would be waiting. They would throw supplies over the wall or jump over the wall with the supplies before the teachers could react.

We had one problem in that most of our vehicles were blockaded within the compound. I wanted to free them and get them out to the Quezon Institute, the Tuberculosis Hospital which we were using as headquarters for our activity. While the teachers were on strike, we were interviewing new teacher candidates at the QI TB facilities. One Sunday, I invited all of our TB out-patients, over a thousand strong, to come to our Boystown for Mass, instead of offering Mass at the QI TB social hall. The TB patients were directly affected by the striking teachers. The teachers had prevented the Sisters, or at least they tried to prevent them, from bringing food, medicine and laundry to our TB patients each day. At first, the teachers set up barbed wire barricades to prevent the TB patients from entering. Some of these TB patients were former commandos, ex-convicts and very tough individuals. The patients immediately destroyed the barbed wire and walked into the compound. Mass went very well. After Mass, we distributed medicine to the patients and the atmosphere was bright and even festive.

Then the Sisters quietly told the patients that we wanted them to clear out the entrance to our compound, so that we could free our vehicles. No sooner said than done. The patients, a thousand strong, marched toward the entrance, tore down the tents, removed all the barricades, and sent the teachers scurrying and running hither and fro in hysteria. Immediately, all our vehicles which were standing by exited. After that we kept them at QI for our needs and service. The scene was one not to be repeated. Imagine a thousand TB patients standing in the middle of the street disrupting and stopping traffic on both sides. They are raising their fists in the air shouting tibak, tibak, which means TB, TB.

However, the day ended on a very unhappy note. Some of the younger patients lingered on to play basketball, after the others had left. When they left later in the afternoon, they were waylaid by some thugs hired by the teachers. They were badly beaten with metal pipes. I went to look at them and was appalled with what I saw. Two patients had their faces badly beaten and were bruised and bloody. We sent them to the hospital where x-rays were taken. They had concussions but nothing serious and after a few days were released. I realized the danger I was running in bringing the TB patients to confront the striking teachers but I had reached the point that I thought it necessary to push the matter to the limit and see where it would take us.

Right after that, another very dramatic episode occurred one night. About one in the morning, just after the teachers who were sleeping in their cots on the sidewalk had turned in, a car driving down the road went out of control. As it turned out the driver had no license and the brakes did not work. The car plowed into the striking teachers. Four or five were badly injured and rushed to the hospital. This was the first time ever, that anything of this nature had occurred. If it had happened an hour before, no one would have been injured because the teachers would not have been in bed. As it turned out, it looked like an act of God to warn the teachers.

Later, when I had a meeting with the teachers, I pointed out to them very calmly that, although I am not a prophet, this episode was strange and fraught with meaning. It is very possible, I said, that the teachers in their misguided zeal and idealism were fighting against God and this was a frightful thought. After that incident, some of the teachers separated themselves from their striking co-workers.

Other teachers accused me in the media of hiring somebody and deliberately perpetrating this act of violence. As time elapsed, I learned that lying and deception were part of the arsenal which the teachers used freely. They would stop at nothing.

Finally, I went to Cardinal Sin and pleaded for his help. My first plea went unheeded. Then I sent the Sisters and they were more successful. The Cardinal contacted President Aquino who contacted one of her generals and asked him to send soldiers to our Boystown/Girlstown. We had twenty or thirty soldiers stationed at our compound for about ten days. This kept the entrance open. During the soldiers stay, we opened another gate and also conducted the annual retreat for the Sisters.

The children had returned. We had hired substitute teachers to replace all those who were on strike. Yet, the strike was continuing. Finally, I decided that enough was enough. It was Pentecost morning. After Mass, I went to the entrance of the compound and spoke to the leader of the strikers who was an ex-seminarian. He was very bright but very misguided. I told him that we would no longer tolerate their presence at the entrance as it was disruptive of our educational program and it created an atmosphere of tension and anxiety which was very harmful to the children. I mentioned that, if they continued, we would meet violence with violence.

During this time, we had formed our little group of commandos from neighboring squatter areas. These were young toughs who were ready and willing and able to do whatever we instructed them to do. Also, we had over a thousand TB outpatients, many of whom were used to violence and afraid of nothing. These two groups were ready to fight back. In addition, we had the parents of the children numbering about eight thousand strong, many of whom were waiting to be called in to assist us. In fact, we had the children themselves, the older boys were very daring and just dying to get involved in the action. I pointed all this out to the leader of the striking teachers and I suggested, "From now on, you and your fellow strikers should sleep very lightly at night."

My words apparently put the fear of the Lord in his heart. In the afternoon, he called and wanted to meet to begin negotiations. We met for one or two days. I agreed to give each striking teacher an extra month's salary and they agreed to pack up and call it quits. Within two days, they were true to their word, although we had to argue and fight all night. Many of the striking teachers were vehemently opposed to the settlement. They wanted to see this strike go to the end. But within two days, the strike was over. The teachers of course, sued and the matter is still in litigation. Our lawyer is called the attorney of eternal delay because he can drag on a case forever. In the Philippines, usually the employer loses the first ruling but then appeals. This takes two or three years. Then if the employer loses the first appeal, he appeals to the Supreme Court. So, the case could drag on for eight or ten years. This would exhaust the teachers and there is every possibility that the final ruling will be in our favor.

In fact the initial ruling of the labor court was in our favor and declared that the teacher's strike was illegal and under the circumstances they were in violation of the law.

These are the highlights of this exciting period. There were many small acts of violence. Rocks and bricks were thrown at us and at our vehicles. Windows were smashed and Sisters were obscenely and violently threatened. They were denounced in the press, on TV, and on the radio. They tried to have the Korean Sisters deported and so on and so on.

However, it was a learning experience for all of the Sisters and great preparation for the future.

For myself, however, it took a terrible toll on my health and after the strike was settled and I returned to Korea, I found myself in something of a physical tailspin. I was losing weight and visibly much weaker than before. I called my doctor in San Francisco, to describe my condition and the symptoms. His advice was to prepare, as it was very possible that in three or four months I would be gone. At the time, I had every reason to follow his advice and believe his prediction.

Fr. Al standing near his room in Pusan, Korea (1965).

Fr. Al cleaning some inmates at the beggars' home in Pusan, Korea (1969).

Fr. Al with his kindergarten children at Pusan, Korea (1970).

Some of the graduates and their families return to Pusan for Father's birthday (1990).

Fr. Al is invested as a Monsignor, February 1, 1990, Manila, Philippines.

Fr. Al in Mexico on his exercise bike, with Sr. Margie and Sr. Jucunda.

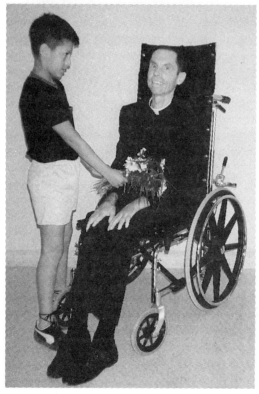

Mexican boy says I
love you with flowers,
Chalco, Mexico, (1991)

During the ordination of Fr. Joseph Kim, a member of the Brothers of Christ; Fr. Al founded this religious group of men, May 10, 1981.

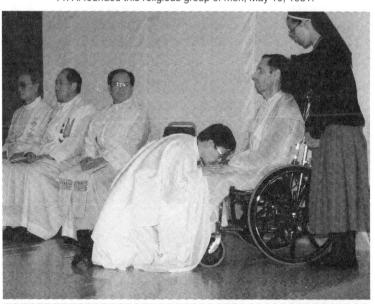

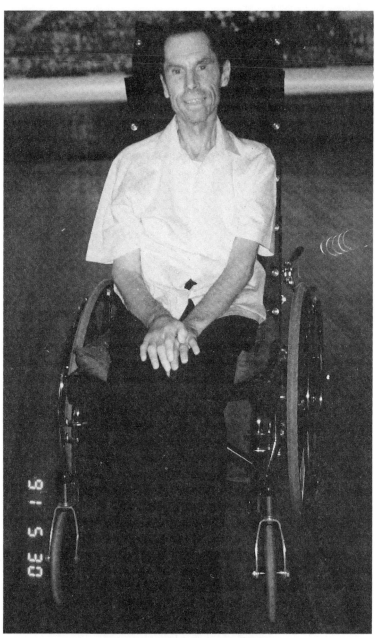

Fr. Al, a year before his death (1991).

Chapter 9

Second Journey to Mexico

I returned to Korea from the Philippines in June 1990. It was obvious that the teachers' strike had taken a heavy toll on my health. I was in something of a physical tailspin. I was losing weight, all my muscles were fibrillating with great gusto, and basically I was exhausted. I felt more dead than alive.

I called my sister, Dolores, and described my symptoms to her. Since the inception of my disease, she has become something of an expert on ALS and she is my best medical adviser. At my suggestion, she called Dr. Norris in San Francisco relating to him what I had told her. She called me back to report what Dr. Norris had to say. It was not cheerful news.

Dr. Norris felt that, perhaps, I had only three or four months left to live. His advice was that I prepare quickly and get everything in order. I asked Sister Monica who was acting as my nurse and attendant at that time, what she thought about the doctor's opinion. She concurred fully with what the doctor had to say. If I continued to deteriorate at the present rate, it was probable that I had only a few months to live.

I felt that the doctor's advice and Sister Monica's opinion reflected the reality of my condition. I also felt that it was very possible I would not make it to my sixtieth birthday on September 18.

The deteriorating state of my health raised new doubts concerning the Mexican project. I had agonized so much over this decision last February and March. I thought that once the decision was made, that was it. But I was mistaken. Once again, I found myself in the darkness of Gethsemane, prostrate on the ground, my face pressed to the earth, sweating blood, and asking the question in my heart, "Is this really the will of the Lord"?

This inner dialogue was very painful. I constantly heard conflicting advice.

"Prudence is better than valor." This sentence from the Scripture is one of my favorites. The Mexican project at this juncture in my life was certainly an undertaking of courage. But, was it prudent; was it the wise thing to do? Looking at the situation objectively, the answer of course was a resounding "No." It seemed to violate every tenet of common sense. It might be the gutsy thing to do but it sure seemed stupid from a human point of view. This did not frighten me. I was never one who was afraid of failure or making a fool of myself. The only thing that concerned me and caused inner torment was the fear that I was following my own will rather than the will of the Lord. I thought of the experience of St. Bernard in the middle ages. At the insistence of a Holy Pope and many learned and pious theologians, St Bernard preached with fire and enthusiasm a crusade to liberate the Holy Land from the Muslims. The heart of his message was, "Deus volit," "the Lord wills it." As it turned out, his crusade which was also sponsored by St. Louis, King of France, another saint, ended as a failure and real disaster. Bernard, a saint advised by saints, and led by saints, ended up by making the wrong decision. I am no St. Bernard or St. Louis or any other kind of saint. So, there was always the slim possibility that I was being deluded and deceived by an inner voice which was my own voice rather than that of Christ or worse yet, the voice of the evil one who is a master of disguise, deception and pretense.

Yet the words of the voice kept arising from my heart. "You begin the project. You don't have to finish it. This will be your Unfinished Symphony." I was not totally convinced but this was the deciding argument. The Missionaries of Guadalupe would back up the sisters and I could launch the project but they would finish it.

In my heart I objected, "But, it will not be what I want or it will not be on a par with what we have set up in Korea and the

Philippines." The answer to this objection was, "The best is the enemy of the good. So what if the project in Mexico will not be perfect, and we have to compromise. It will be good and achieve something for the glory of God, even if it is not to be the best."

Going back and forth, blowing hot one day, cold the next, I finally decided to return to Mexico. I wanted Sister Elena and Sister Cecille to accompany me. They are the two sisters from the Philippines who were to be pioneers in the Mexican project. My health was unsteady and I felt very shaky on my own. However, the sisters could not get visas in time, so, I went on my own.

Following my instructions, Damiano went to the Korean Air Lines office. He asked if wheelchair service was available. He told them I was having difficulty in walking and standing in line was very painful. He made the mistake of telling the doctor in charge of the medical department of KAL that I had ALS. The doctor upon hearing I had ALS pushed a panic button. Very recently, the doctor said, another airline had great difficulty with an ALS patient when it was aloft. The patient was in critical condition. He had great difficulty in breathing and there was a question whether the plane would have to turn around and abort its flight. I discovered later that he was referring to the president of the Goldstar Company who was a victim of ALS. He was dying and he went to San Francisco for emergency medical treatment via another major carrier. He had great difficulty in breathing and he was a source of serious concern to the captain of the plane and the airline authorities. So, the doctor was legitimately concerned. He said I would have to have a thorough medical exam before they would allow me to travel, let alone, afford me the wheelchair service which I had requested. Luckily, Damiano did not divulge my name and told them to forget the whole matter.

When I arrived at the counter to check in for my flight to Mexico, I was apprehensive. As it turned out, they had somehow traced me and knew I was an ALS patient. The girl behind the counter asked if I wanted wheelchair service. Happily, I said, "No, I can make it very easily on my own." But my name had been flagged in their computer and as soon as I checked in, word was sent to the airline authorities.

I was in the waiting lounge with the other passengers quietly waiting for the announcement to board the aircraft. My name was announced over the loudspeaker. I was instructed to report to the information desk for an urgent matter. I ignored the announcement and remained in the waiting lounge. Very quickly, two airline authorities found me in the lounge and began inquiring about the state of my health. I said there was no problem, I had arthritis, which is very true, and that was why I wanted the wheelchair but not to worry, I was in fine shape.

From their expressions, I could see they did not buy my story. They left and shortly afterwards, another official came and began to interrogate me. After he left, I saw a group of people approaching the waiting area. Several of these people appeared to be medical personnel because they were wearing white coats and carrying kits which looked like they contained medical equipment. They headed straight for me. I had become the object of curiosity of all the other waiting passengers. The medical personnel opened their medical paraphernalia and said they had to conduct a medical exam before they would permit me to board the aircraft. At this, I put on a great display of anger, even though I was very much in control, and my outburst was only for show. In a voice loud enough for all the other passengers to hear, I asked, since when did they have a regulation demanding that a passenger submit to a medical exam before he could board the aircraft. I would submit to this exam on one condition and that was that every passenger undergo a similar test. I had taken a medical exam in Pusan a few days before. At that time, my blood pressure was irregular and my pulse was very rapid. I knew if I submitted myself to an exam, they would never let me board the aircraft.

At this, the boarding announcement was heard over the loudspeaker. I ignored the medical people and airline authorities and took my place in line with the other passengers. They were visibly confused and bamboozled. In my own mind I said if they want to keep me from boarding that aircraft, they would have to do it by physical force. They would have to drag me from the plane, kicking and screaming. They let me board the aircraft but it was not until the plane had started to move and the aircraft was aloft that I was at ease and felt that I was truly on my way to Mexico. The incident was bizarre and even humorous. It seemed that an evil force was doing its best to keep me from moving ahead with this Mexican project.

About ten days later, on my way back from Mexico, I changed planes in Los Angeles. I had a return reservation but the airline authorities had canceled it unbeknownst to me. So, again, I had to fight with the agents to get my name reinstated and to get back on the plane for Korea.

While in Mexico City, I lodged at the seminary of the Missionaries of Guadalupe. They received me into their community as a brother. I was touched by their warmth and support and genuine interest in what I was planning to do. This was my second taste of community life since my ordination to the priesthood more than thirty years before. The first, was with the Carmelites in Washington, D.C. I found this brief taste of community life sweet and pleasant. But I realized my vocation was more like that of John the Baptist. I was called to be a loner. It was a painful calling. Many times over the years, I thought I would die of loneliness and solitude. But certainly it was God's Providence. Only a loner could do what I was called to do. I will not develop this theme further but I believe it is a simple fact of reality.

The Superior General was extremely accommodating. Upon his invitation, I offered community Mass for the seminarians concelebrated by all the priests. I gave a talk in English explaining my work. The rector of the seminary translated it into Spanish.

During my stay, Father Hector and I looked at various land sites which were for sale which might be suitable for our Boystown project. The one we saw on the last day of my stay was the one which I chose. It was located in Chalco and was 35 hectares. You can measure one kilometer from the beginning of the property to the end and it averaged 360 meters across. It was rectangularly shaped and surrounded by trees and a fence. It had a road, good water and also a beautiful hacienda at the front of the property. In the background were the two most beautiful snow covered volcanoes not only in Mexico but in the world. It was a beautiful piece of land, which I was told was previously owned by the former President of Mexico. The present owner was a well known singer and actor. I told Father Hector to begin negotiations to purchase this property. My only reservation was that perhaps it was too big.

But then I thought, Mexico City is the biggest city in the world and the value of the property would increase with each passing year.

During my stay at the seminary, I spoke with the Superior General. I formally asked his society to loan Father Hector to work with me on a year's trial basis. I told the Superior General of my medical problem and said if the answer was no, I would not be devastated. In fact, I would be elated. I would interpret a negative answer as a sign that it was not God's will for me to go ahead with the project and would happily abandon it. I said there was no way I could do this alone.

The Superior General met with his council and the answer was a hundred percent positive. So, the Mexican project, despite my many misgivings and halfhearted attempts to pull out, kept moving ahead more or less on its own momentum.

Chapter 10

Third Journey to Mexico

It was now August, 1990 and I was in the Philippines. I kept having second thoughts about the Mexican project mainly because of my deteriorating health.

I called in Sisters Elena and Cecille who had volunteered to head this mission. I told them, "Today, carry on this project without me." I told them to think carefully as it was very possible I would not be around to help them in a few months. Could they do it without me? They both answered with great faith and courage, "Yes, Father, we can." This put me in mind of the answer of James and John when Jesus asked the question, "Can you drink of my chalice?" "Yes, we can." But as it turned out, when the chalice was put to the lips of James, he turned and ran like a coward.

The sisters answered with faith and courage but without the full awareness of what they were saying. Later, as things turned out, they were very frightened on their own. When confronted with the enormity of the Mexican responsibility, they trembled and shook with doubt.

However, they kept urging me to pursue this project because they believe the church is weak and that we offer something original and fresh.

Sometime before, I had in passing asked Cardinal Sin his opinion. He dismissed the Mexican project with a wave of his hand saying, "Forget about Mexico, there is so much you can do here in the Philippines." This was another very strong argument against Mexico. Why go to Mexico where the problems and difficulties are new and enormous? Why not focus on the Philippines, where I know the problems and can do so much more? Besides the costs of programs in the Philippines would be much cheaper than in Mexico. There are perhaps 500,000–600,000 Filipino youth who would qualify for entry into our Boystown and Girlstown. Why not simply develop our projects in the Philippines and forget about distant lands and distant places.

I decided to send Sister Elena and Sister Cecille to see Cardinal Sin without me and ask his opinion again. I was convinced he would still be opposed. The sisters came back and reported to my amazement that the Cardinal strongly urged us to go ahead with this venture. He said we have a special charisma that he had come to recognize and certainly we could do marvels for the Church and wonders for Christ by going ahead with this project. This advice was totally unexpected.

Shortly thereafter, I was in Cebu, in the Philippines, supervising construction. I called on Cardinal Vidal. I also asked his opinion concerning my Mexican plans. Secretly I hoped he would dismiss this as a hair-brain idea. He laughed and said, "Go ahead with it, it is a great idea," and he pointed to the wall behind me which was facing him at his desk. I turned around to see what he was pointing at. To my surprise, it was a huge painting of Our Lady of Guadalupe. She was looking over my shoulder and he was looking at her laughing. In effect, he was saying, "She is calling you, do not hesitate, go!"

So it seemed the harder I tried to get out of the project the more I got boxed in and drawn to it. Sisters Elena and Cecille finally succeeded in getting their U.S. and Mexican visas. We made plans to leave the Philippines at the end of August, spend a few days in Korea, and then go on to Mexico together. We were scheduled to leave the Philippines on a Friday. On Wednesday, I developed a serious backache. It was so painful, I could not straighten up and I had great difficulty walking or standing. The sisters were greatly alarmed. The fact that my difficulties came at the eleventh hour, made things very dramatic. Everything indicated that this was a sign from God to abandon this Mexican scheme. I was in no state to travel, so I decided to at least put the Mexican project on hold.

I called Father Hector Diaz in Mexico City to explain that I could hardly walk and was in no state to travel. I told him that I had decided to put the Mexican project on hold until June after our construction in Silang, Cavite, Philippines was completed. If by that time, I was still around and still able to function, I would reconsider the Mexican venture. He said that he believed if we hesitated now we would not get started again. We had already started things in motion, the momentum was with us, and if we stopped many people would lose confidence in us. He strongly urged me to go ahead with the project. His strongest argument went something like this, "Father, the ballplayers can play even without the manager." What in effect he was saying was, "We can handle it without you."

I finally decided to put the matter to the judgment of the medical experts. I called Dr. Norris in San Francisco. I had already outlined my plans for Mexico. I gave him a description, as best as I could, of my physical condition. I told him I was hesitating whether to go ahead with the Mexican venture. I had to have a better than fifty percent chance of staying alive for at least two years, with at least a fifty percent chance of being functional. Based on your experience, intuition and expertise what would you advise me? There was a long pause. Finally, Dr. Norris said, "Go for it!"

"Go for it!" These words were ringing in my ears but I could hardly go two steps unaided because of the state of my back. But to my surprise, the next day after some hand massages, physical therapy and a little exercise, I began to feel a little better. So, the two sisters and I with my aching back boarded the plane as planned for Korea. And then a few days later, we went to Mexico.

It was a happy trip. The sisters were like children. They were bright, cheerful and courageous. We stopped off in San Francisco overnight. I had an appointment with some of the ALS experts. Also, the next morning, we paid a memorable visit to Charlie Wedemeyer, a famous U.S. athlete who has been afflicted with ALS for more than ten years now. Charlie, a remarkable individual and the reigning hero of ALS patients, is on a ventilator and has not eaten for five years except through a tube in his stomach. He has remained extremely cheerful, positive and active. Maybe I will devote a chapter of this book to Charlie's story.

I arrived in Mexico City late in the evening with the two sisters in tow. Father Hector Diaz escorted the sisters to a nearby convent where the sisters offered their hospitality to the Sisters of Mary on a temporary basis. I stayed at the seminary.

The sisters who are used to the warm, tropical Philippine climate found the cold of Mexico City very hard to endure. They related the next morning that they were so cold at night they went to bed with their shoes and stockings on.

I was becoming weaker and weaker, so as arranged, the sisters came to the seminary each morning to assist me in getting dressed and ready for the day. Then I would go off to Mass with the two sisters and we would go together to have breakfast with the seminarians.

A few days after my arrival, Father Hector came to me with a startling revelation, the rector of their university and twice selected former Superior General of the order was interested in the land purchase. He enjoined and enlisted the services of his nephew, who was an attorney and a real estate agent. The nephew was an interesting character who looked very much like a river boat gambler. Father Hector told me the nephew came to him with a scam to swindle me out of a million dollars in the course of the land purchase.

"How much do you think Father is willing to pay for the land," asked the nephew? "About 3 million," replied Father Hector. "I can get it for 2 million and we will split the difference, five hundred thousand for you and five hundred thousand for me." Father Hector's eyes widened and his face registered surprise. But the nephew shrugged and said, "You can always use it for your missionary work in Korea."

Father Hector took this matter to the uncle. The uncle listened to it calmly, shrugged his shoulders and in effect said, "That's the way it's done here. So, what else is new?" In other words, the uncle had tacitly approved of a conspiracy to swindle us out of a large sum of money.

I spent two or three sleepless nights thinking about this matter. I said to myself, if I cannot trust these priests who are supposed to back up this project and carry it through when I'm no longer around, I cannot go ahead with it. I was seriously thinking of getting on the next plane with the two sisters and going back to Korea and the Philippines. We had not yet passed the point of no return.

However, I saw so much genuine charity and brotherly love among the priests and the students of the seminary that I thought truly the spirit of the Lord is here. This led me to decide despite the swindle scheme to go ahead with the Mexican venture. (Later we managed to recover most of the money.)

A corporation was set up and the land purchase contract was written. I was running around meeting contractors and builders. Finally, a contractor was contacted and he asked for a hundred thousand dollars to get started immediately. I hesitated. I knew once the check had been written for a hundred thousand and put into his hands, we would have passed the point of no return. Finally, I decided to go ahead with it, wrote the check, and gave it to him for better or for worse. We had burned our bridges and now there was no turning back.

I was scheduled to leave Mexico on the morning of September 18, my sixtieth birthday. Sisters Elena and Cecille entered my room about five in the morning and I was still in bed. They came to my bedside, sang Happy Birthday, gave me a rose, a lovely painting and a greeting that they had designed. It was very touching. We went together to the airport and I boarded the seven o'clock plane for Los Angeles and then went on to Seoul, Korea. As I was leaving, I felt I would never be back again. I told the sisters that this might be our final meeting. I have said this three or four times since then. Somehow, I've been able to return.

Also, I failed to mention one of the first visits I make whenever I arrive in Mexico and the last before I leave is to the Shrine of Our Lady of Guadalupe. She is the one who is responsible for this project and so each opportunity I get, I remind her of her responsibility and reconsecrate the project, the sisters and myself to her loving care.

Chapter 11

Sixty Years

My sixtieth birthday celebration in Korea deserves at least a page or two in this book. As mentioned in the previous chapter, the real date of my birth is September 18, 1930. However, in agreement with the Sisters, I had decided to formally celebrate my birthday on September 27, which is also the Korean "Chusukansajol," or Thanksgiving Day. I planned to use my sixtieth birthday celebration to encourage our Boystown and Girlstown graduates to be faithful to the principles and values we had taught them and to play on their emotions in order to stimulate them spiritually.

First of all, it should be explained that in the Orient in general and in Korea in particular, one's sixtieth birthday is not just another birthday. It is a very special occasion. In the past the life expectancy was very short and it was considered a great accomplishment for one to live sixty years. So, the event was celebrated with great pomp and ceremony. The sixtieth birthday in Korea, which is called "hwaekap," is really the fourth of July, Christmas and the Super Bowl all welded into one.

We had announced through our Boystown and Girlstown newsletter to all our alumni that there would be a celebration. We invited each and every one to come to Pusan to join in the festivities. I asked each graduate to prepare for this special occasion by reviewing his or her spiritual life, getting their religious life in order, and making a good confession. If their marital state was not proper, I asked that they take care of this before my sixtieth birthday. My graduates responded very favorably. They had meetings, spiritual colloquies, and by and large my request had a very positive effect on their overall spiritual and religious life.

For me, the birthday celebration was something of a burden. Each day I was feeling more and more fatigued, but if it was useful for the troops, I said, well, let's give it a try and do our best.

It should be pointed out, that the general reaction of my boys and girls to my ALS affliction was based on Korean tradition and a mixture of superstition and Shintoist belief. The view of affliction in the Old Testament, or for that matter, the view of affliction by most of the Pharisees at the time of Christ, even the disciples of Christ shared this view, is evidenced when the man who was blind from birth was brought to Jesus to be cured, the question was asked, "Lord, who has sinned, this man or his parents?" Jesus answered of course, "Neither has sinned but this affliction is for the glory of God."

Somehow, my boys and girls thought that maybe they had sinned and if they were to live more fervently and more virtuously God would reconsider His decision and restore me to health. So, the disease in my body had a very positive effect on the morale and the spiritual life of my children. They all were doing their very best to live good lives. They were praying as never before. Indeed, I joked, if I had realized what the effect of this illness would have on the day to day lives of my children, even if God did not send it to me in a real manner, I would have invented it long before this.

The first sixtieth birthday celebration was held in Seoul. The Sisters and the children put on an outstanding musical program. When I was in the U.S. going through the medical tests to determine the nature of my affliction, I mentioned offhandedly to my sister, Dolores, that among my favorite songs were "When the Saints Go Marching In" and "Shenandoah, How I Love You." Dolores found tapes and music of these two songs and sent them to the Sisters in Korea. So, throughout the celebration, both in Seoul and Pusan, these two songs kept popping up.

I was very touched and really had to fight to hold back the tears, especially in Pusan, as the Sisters and the choir of children

were singing, "When The Saints Go Marching In" with great
enthusiasm and verve. One of the girl students, who was dressed
like St. Therese of Lisieux in Carmelite garb, came down from the
stage and presented me with a bouquet of flowers. This might
sound a little schmaltzy, but it was genuinely moving and touching. I had to look away to hold back the tears.

In passing, it should be pointed out that one of the features
of ALS is that the patient frequently has increasing difficulty in
controlling his emotions. The facial muscles which control the
eyes and the shedding of tears are weak. Frequently, an ALS
patient suffers from what I believe is called, "lability," which
means uncontrolled fits of weeping or laughing. I have never, to
date, experienced this but I do have increasing difficulty controlling tears and also regulating my laughter.

The celebration in Seoul was moving. The one in Pusan,
however, was the highlight of the birthday bash. I had insisted
that it be strictly an in-house family celebration. So, only members
of our immediate family, the children, the alumni, teachers and
workers and, of course, the Sisters and Brothers attended with a
few exceptions. And more than a thousand of our alumni came for
the Mass and the musical/dramatic program in the evening.
Many came with their spouses and children.

Mass, which was the high point of the day, was celebrated at
eleven in the morning in the new gymnasium and assembly hall
which had just recently been completed. The scene at Mass and the
musical accompaniment were outstanding. At Mass, I gave a
sermon in which I thanked all those who came for the celebration.
I mentioned that my heart was overflowing with gratitude to God
for all the graces and gifts which He had showered upon me over
a period of sixty years. The three greatest graces among so many,
were, first, the grace of good, pious, religious parents; two, the
grace of a priestly and missionary vocation; and third, the grace of
the ALS affliction.

These words sounded lofty and saintly at the time they were
spoken and they came from the heart. But now, it is much later in
the development of ALS and I am not sure if I had to give that
sermon again if I would speak of ALS as one of the greatest gifts

and graces of my life. I would say, "I would like the courage to look upon this affliction as a grace. I would like the spirit of faith to consider this disease as a gift from God."

To be strictly objective at this point, knowing by experience the pain and suffering with ALS, if God were to send an angel who presented me with two options; one, I could choose ALS with all its pain and suffering, or; two, I could choose my former health, although, it was never robust; it was functional and served me well, I know I should practice all the indifference and say, "Lord, you do the choosing. You know what is best for me. I do not know." I should practice this holy surrender of St. Francis de Sales, who expresses it with the words, "Ask for nothing, refuse nothing." I should practice the sacrament of the present moment, accept from day to day, moment to moment, whatever the Lord chooses.

I know this should be my attitude. However, if at this point I were presented with these two options, I would be sorely tempted to look away from the ALS, saying something like this, "Lord, I know that the affliction is a gift from you who chastises whom You love. This is a mark of your special love but you also know of what I am made, that I am made only of dust and clay. You know how lacking I am in patience, in courage, and in determination. So, really, if it is all the same to you, I would prefer to give this grace to someone much stronger and more patient than myself. As it is, I have enough difficulty in practicing patience with my present body and physical condition."

In all honesty, unless the spirit of the Lord gave me special inspiration and courage at this time, I would be very reluctant to receive ALS as a choice of grace and a gift to be desired. All of this is, perhaps, an indication of a lack of faith, but honesty compels me to tell it like it is and if the truth is to be known, that's the way it is.

The sixtieth birthday celebration was a success from every point of view. A couple of months previously I had serious doubts whether I would make it to my sixtieth birthday. But, I not only made it to the date in question but survived with great joy and rejoicing.

Chapter 12

Subsequent Journeys to Mexico

W hen I left Mexico in September of 1990, in my heart I was convinced I would not be back again. This conviction was in my heart each time I left Mexico. As it turned out, to my surprise, I did return. In fact, I made three more trips to Mexico. I will summarize these three journeys to Mexico in one chapter.

In late November, I returned to Mexico and I spent two or three weeks there. This time I did not stay in the seminary, but I lodged in our own house, on our own property. I was not too interested in including the purchase of the villa with the property, but the Guadalupe Father who was negotiating the land purchase transaction was adamant. He insisted that unless the villa was sold with the property, there would be no sale. As it turned out, the procurement of the villa was providential.

This became our base of operations for the next ten months until the Boystown and Girlstown buildings were ready and we could move into them. It proved to be a very convenient and useful headquarters. It was extremely attractive. The villa was designed by one of the most distinguished architects in all of Mexico. It was really a work of art both outside and inside; every detail was carefully planned, designed and the finished results can only be described as exquisite in beauty. The furniture came with the house as well as the telephone which proved to be not only useful but essential to our program.

Among other things, the villa gave us credibility which was certainly needed. Many people in high places in the Church and government were very skeptical when we discussed our plans for our Boystown and Girlstown complex which would be totally free and which would serve, exclusively, children who were the poorest and the most destitute. They listened to our grandiose plans. They looked at the three sisters, all very young, very small and very foreign, two from the Philippines and one from Korea, and our words raised a big fat question mark in their minds and in their eyes. But when they visited our property and saw the impressive villa, many of these same people were won over. The villa also became a base of operations for interviewing candidates for the Sisters of Mary, prospective teachers, and also parents and children who were applying for admission to the Boystown and Girlstown.

Attached to the villa were a number of buildings (i.e. sheds or warehouses) which we renovated in the Spring and converted into dormitory and classroom facilities. We accepted 90 children, 45 boys and 45 girls and this became our pilot project. This enabled the sisters to get experience working with Mexican children for two or three months before the large influx in September. Also, it helped the sisters train leaders among the Mexican children who would help with the main group when they arrived in September. It was a marvelous pilot project which turned out to be very beneficial.

I left Mexico on the feast of Our Lady of Guadalupe, December 12, 1990 in order to be in Korea for Christmas. After Christmas I wanted to be available for the annual retreat and renewal of vows by the sisters and graduation for the children.

Originally, a Guadalupe Father was scheduled to accompany me on my trip back to Korea. I was growing weaker and weaker and it was a risk to travel alone. However, as it turned out, it was decided that the Mexican priest would be more helpful if he remained in Mexico. We were working on our pamphlets and posters to send to the Parish priests, in an attempt to recruit Mexican candidates for the Sisters of Mary. He was needed to complete this important assignment. So, I decided with a great deal of apprehension to try the trip on my own.

Actually I was not on my own. I felt that Our Lady of Guadalupe was accompanying me. In my heart, I kept repeating the marvelous gentle words of Mary to Juan Diego, "Do not be afraid. Am I not here? Are you not in my heart? Will anything be lacking to you?"

When I arrived at the airport in Mexico City, it was very early in the morning and very cold. I was shivering as I waited in my wheelchair. Sister Cecille was busy pounding and massaging me in an attempt to get me warmed up for the trip. Sister Elena was busy checking me in with the airlines and Sister Margie was engaged in deep, serious conversation with a Korean man and a group of young Korean women. I was not sure who they were nor what Sister Margie was up to.

When I got on the plane, the young Korean women came to me and introduced themselves. The older man was the leader of the group. It was a group of Korean folk dancers who had been on tour in Mexico and were now returning to their home country. They said that Sister Margie had instructed them to look after me and I was not to worry. So, they did their best to assist me in little ways on the leg of the trip from Mexico to San Francisco.

The real test, of course, was from San Francisco to Seoul. This was a genuine test of stamina. The trip usually lasted twelve to thirteen hours. I walked into the plane struggling to keep my balance supported by a cane in my left hand. The chief stewardess immediately came to me and personally escorted me to my seat. She inquired concerning my ailment and took a very deep maternal interest in my situation. As it turned out, she had a son who was afflicted with some type of similar ailment. So, she had a great deal of sympathy for one in my predicament. She gave instructions to the other stewardesses to take special care of me. They did their best to make me comfortable and to help me.

When I left the plane, I left in a wheelchair. The chief stewardess came to me in front of all the other stewardesses and pilots and she planted a kiss on my forehead and presented me with a bottle of very expensive champagne wrapped in a towel, as a personal gift. I was very touched and I felt like someone who had won the Wimbledon tennis cup. I had finished the course and I, with the help of Our Lady of Guadalupe, made it to Korea on my own; although, all the sisters and everyone who knew me were very concerned and full of dire warnings and predictions. At the same time, I felt a bit foolish being wheeled through Kimpo Airport with this bottle of champagne on my lap. I uncorked the champagne at Christmas and drank some of its contents with the Apostolic Nuncio, Archbishop Diaz, who was my guest on that occasion.

While in Korea, I was in constant contact with Mexico by telephone. In March, 1991 I had the feeling it was time to go back, that I was needed. This time I was no longer able to travel alone. I brought my Filipino architect with me and a Korean sister, Sister Jucunda, who was serving as my nurse and attendant.

This proved to be my longest stay in Mexico. Originally, I was scheduled to stay for only two or three weeks. However, there were a lot of loose ends to tie up. I was convinced I would not be back again. So, I purposely extended my stay. As it turned out, I remained more than six weeks; in fact, I spent Holy Week, Easter and the week after Easter in Mexico.

We were way behind on our construction schedule. Mexico is the land of mañana. Mexico is a land of empty promises and I began to wonder if there was any way possible we could get these buildings ready for September, which was our target date and the time when the school year started. Also, there were a lot of misgivings about finances. Our architect and contractor had been highly recommended by the priests of the Missionaries of Guadalupe. In fact, he was the brother-in-law of one of the priests. But Mexican contractors have a very bad reputation for honesty. In fact, they are famous for their ability to exploit those for whom they work.

So much money had been paid, so much money was going out and so little was being done. It was frightening. I had my architect, accountant, and lawyer go over all the receipts and try to get a hold on the finances. Also, I tried to build a fire under the contractor. Eventually, he did get moving and things began to pick up steam.

As for finances, I have to admit the first phase of construction cost two or three times more than what was promised and more than what was expected. But, there is no way that I could have done it any differently and, at the same time, moved ahead so aggressively and rapidly. If I had a five year plan and it was not pushed by any sense of urgency, it is possible I could have done it cheaper and better. But here again, I am not too certain of that.

During my stay, I preached a retreat to the three sisters and also witnessed their annual renewal of vows. The Bishop was invited. He came out and blessed the construction and had dinner with us. He became extremely involved and most supportive of our work. Since then, he has come to visit the sisters and the children on many occasions. He has spoken of us with lavish praise to his fellow Mexican Bishops and, in fact, he has given us a statue of the Sacred Heart for our Boystown which the Holy Father gave him as his personal gift.

We sent letters, flyers and posters to all the parishes explaining the nature of the Sisters of Mary and asking for recruits. The response was extremely meager. I have been told that vocations were numerous in Mexico. I have been told the same thing about the Philippines. My experience is that vocations to a group which serves the poor, such as the Sisters of Mary, in the spirit of sacrifice and hard work, are extremely few and far between. We received so many inquiries, so many young women visiting us but very few real applicants or candidates. In fact, after a year's worth of recruiting, advertising, and soliciting, we now have only three Mexican aspirants. But these three look very good and hopefully they are the nucleus of our Mexican Sisters of Mary. I personally feel that the bulk of our future candidates will come from the graduates of our own school system. These will be children trained by the sisters and brought up in their spirit. So, we will have to wait a few years for this. This has been my experience in the Philippines.

Since there were so few sisters and the prospect of recruiting from among the Mexican young people seemed unpromising, I decided to enlist the help of our Filipino graduates of our Boystown and Girlstown. We enlisted 15 volunteers, 7 boys and 8 girls. These were from our first group of graduates and they were currently working in our Boystown and Girlstown in the Philippines. They enthusiastically accepted our proposal to go to Mexico to work as lay volunteers with the sisters. They were given lessons in Spanish for several months and then in June they went to Mexico. They trained with the ninety Mexican children in our pilot project which we began in July. These helping brothers and sisters, as we call them, turned out to be a true Godsend. In fact, without them, there was no way we could function in Mexico.

On Easter Monday the Apostolic Delegate came for Mass and dinner. It was a delightful visit. He, too, was very excited and enthusiastic to learn of our project and our program. He said he would report to the President of Mexico concerning our program. He said what we proposed to do was badly needed for the Mexican society and, especially, for the Church in Mexico. He felt the timing was perfect. The relationship between government and church was being eased and instead of being at odds with each other, they were now becoming more and more friendly and everything looked good for a program such as ours.

I left Mexico in early May, 1991. Again I said farewell with the feeling this would be my last visit to the land of Our Lady of Guadalupe.

As it turned out, again, I was mistaken.

At the end of September 1991, I went back to Mexico to attend the Inauguration of our Boystown and Girlstown which was scheduled for Monday, October 7, the feast of Our Lady of the Rosary. The construction fell way behind in the schedule. I had a meeting, as soon as I arrived, with the contractor and confronted the issue. I announced I had been dedicating buildings for 25 years and never inaugurated a building which was not yet completed except for this one in Mexico. Although many dignitaries and high officials had been notified and had promised to come, I was going to call off the inauguration.

The contractor and his architect were stunned by this announcement. There was a pause, and then he pleaded with me to give them a chance. He said he would work day and night to get everything ready for a memorable inauguration. I agreed to give them a chance and to my surprise and amazement, he and his people did an outstanding job. They worked day and night and even on Sunday and the gym and the workshop and the main building were almost totally completed on the day of the dedication.

The dedication was a triumph. These events can go either

way. They can be a disaster or they can be something spectacular. This was something spectacular and I think this was simply another little taste of honey which the Lord gives me now and then with a bit of medicine which comes afterwards.

The dedication was the longest on record. It lasted about three hours and was divided into two parts The first half was the civil ceremony with speeches, dances, and songs, a tour of the facility and a little snack. This was followed by Concelebrated Mass with the Bishop and his priests, which in turn was followed by dinner.

We had received over eight hundred children. They had been with us only six weeks, but, already, they looked like our children. They were disciplined, bright, cheerful and very impressive. The facilities and the buildings were very, very attractive. All the guests were most impressed and they had lavish praise for the sisters and those associated with the program.

In my heart, I spoke a little muchas gracias to Our Lady of Guadalupe who made all this possible. Mexico was to be my Unfinished Symphony, but, at least, the first movement of the symphony was finished; and this was a cause of great joy, celebration and thanksgiving.

I was reluctant to stay in Mexico too long for fear I would become too weak and I would not be able to get back to Korea or the Philippines, where, I felt I was more needed and more useful. So, I left Mexico at the end of October, 1991 in the company of two sisters. This time as I left Mexico, I was convinced this truly was my last visit.

Before leaving, I made arrangements for the completion of the second phase of the project which would be a replica of the first. The contractor was performing much better and we had much tighter control of finances.

We made many mistakes in our first phase of construction, but, considering everything, progress was remarkable. Within a period of less than eighteen months, I had come to Mexico, and, with the help of three sisters and the grace of God, we purchased land, set up a corporation and obtained construction and education permits. We hired teachers, recruited Mexican candidates, rounded up 800 needy children and completed and inaugurated the buildings, and, we were off and running. This in itself was a minor miracle which took place in the land of mañana.

Chapter 13

The Sacrament of Suffering

I n the Gospel, Jesus says, "If I be lifted up from the earth and raised on high, I would draw all men to myself." Jesus on the cross has drawn my heart to his heart in suffering and pain. These two hearts become one in a very deep and mysterious but real manner.

Pain and suffering accepted in a spirit of faith and love can be likened to the Sacrament of the Eucharist. They unite the one who experiences them in a special way with Christ nailed to the cross. Jesus, in speaking of the Eucharist, says, "Whoever eats my body and drinks my blood is in me and I am in him." These words can be applied to pain and suffering accepted for Christ. Whoever experiences this pain and this suffering is in Christ and Christ is in him. The pain and the suffering are in a way lessened. Pain is pain and suffering is suffering no matter how deep the faith, how bright the hope and how pure the love. At the same time, in the depths of the pain there is this oneness of spirits, and in the heart of the suffering there is this union of souls. And from this oneness and this union there rises a very pure, spiritual peace — this peace of God which surpasses all human understanding.

In the Gospel, Jesus says, "You have not chosen me. I have chosen you and anointed you that you bear fruit, and that your fruit may remain." It is not I who have chosen the Crucified Christ and who have opted to share in this pain and make up in my own body the sufferings which are lacking to His. Before I experienced the terrible pain and horrible suffering associated with this ALS thing, I could think about pain in a romantic manner and speak of suffering in a rather abstract, theoretical fashion. But, after experiencing ALS, if left to myself, I would be hard put to have the courage to deliberately choose it, to select it and opt for it. I am familiar with the episode in the life of St. John of the Cross kneeling at the foot of the crucifix in the chapel. One day, Christ spoke to him and said, "My son, you have done much for my honor. What would you like as a reward?" John answers without hesitation, "Lord, to suffer and to be despised." St. John of the Cross was granted his wish and he suffered greatly before his death and was made the butt of great humiliation. I wonder if John of the Cross would have said in a very concrete, specific manner, "Lord, I would like ALS with all its physical pain, torture and humiliation." Here, again, I am filled with a sense of shame. Do I really think I am made of the same stuff as a John of the Cross? The answer of course is, "No." John was a man of heroic patience, courage and extraordinary determination which goes hand-in-hand with sanctity. I have no doubt that John would have said the same words to Christ, even if it meant this terrible, devastating disease which is ALS.

St. Paul writes in one of his Epistles, "With Christ I am nailed to the cross. It is no longer I who live but Christ who lives in me." These were always among my favorite lines from the writings of St. Paul. Now, they have a special, personal, experiential meaning for me. I believe, in all truthfulness, I can now say with St. Paul, with Christ I am nailed to the cross.

There are so many elements of ALS which remind you of the pain of Jesus nailed to the cross. First of all, Jesus was totally disabled and immobilized. His hands and feet were rigidly fixed to the tree so that He could not move. My condition is now the same. I am totally disabled and can no longer move my hands or feet. On the cross, because of His position and the weight of His body, Jesus had great difficulty in breathing. In fact, he died of suffocation. My breathing now is way below 50 percent of normal. More than likely, I will die of suffocation or choking or something close to respiratory failure which is a clinical description of the cause of the death of Jesus.

Also, Jesus experienced that terrible, overwhelming fatigue

which comes from a lack of rest and sleep. He had not slept the night before and he had gone through terrible pain and torture. Because of the lack of oxygen and many other problems which cause insomnia, an ALS patient is always fatigued and experiences terrible sleepiness and drowsiness. Because of his inability to breathe, Jesus spoke very little from the cross. In fact, only seven words are recorded and they are very brief. Most ALS patients when they die, have lost their ability to speak, not so much from a lack of oxygen as to the fact that their speaking muscles have atrophied. On the cross, Jesus did not drink or eat. He had no taste for any human nutriment. ALS patients have enormous difficulty in swallowing anything and as for myself the sight and thought of food repulses and even nauseates me. Also on Calvary, Jesus was stripped of his clothes. He was stripped of his human dignity and lifted up before the world as a spectacle and a laughing stock. I, too, have been stripped of my dignity. Each day is a new and fresh humiliation.

Oh Jesus, forgive me, for what I am going to say, but I am guilty of entertaining the thought, so, I will express it, in all simplicity and candor. At times I looked at your pain and compared it to my own. Then I said, "Your pain lasted only 15 hours or so, from midnight on Holy Thursday until three on the following Friday afternoon." Indeed the pain was excruciating, the suffering was horrible, but still the time factor is only 15 hours. If I had my choice of enduring 15 hours of your pain on Calvary in exchange for 15 days of ALS, I would choose the 15 hours of Gethsemane and Calvary. I imagine in my daydreaming 15 days of normal, healthy, active existence. So every 15 days, I would have my hands and feet pierced and be stretched out on the cross and then the rest of the time I would be free and happy and healthy. It seems to me, if I had my choice, I would choose the cross in exchange for the ALS pain.

ALS is a fine disease. It has many things to recommend it. It has a nice manly sound to it. There is something even athletic to the idea of Lou Gehrig's disease. Also, it is highly visible and wins a lot of sympathy for you. It is relatively clean and odorless. But the most difficult feature, at least for me, with ALS is that it is so terribly slow. It kills, but so softly, so lazily. If it is going to kill you, let it do it quickly and get it over with. But it is like a cat that has caught a mouse and tortures the mouse by playing with it forever.

Of course, Lord Jesus, when I speak about exchanging my little pain for your suffering, I do not know what I am talking about. I realize I am speaking nonsense and I ask your pardon.

In Scripture, it is written, "Is there any pain like unto my pain?" in reference to the suffering of Jesus. The answer to this question is, "No." Jesus is not only man but God. So His pain is theandric, the pain of the God-man. So there is an element of mystery and an element of infinitude in the pain of Jesus. It is bottomless and it has no ceiling. So really, there is no pain like unto the pain of Jesus.

As to the time factor, this too is misleading. With God there is no time. In the words of St. Peter, "A thousand years are as a day and a day as a thousand years." In this sense then, Jesus, you hung on the cross not just for three hours but for about two hundred years, if a day is as a thousand years in the sight of God and you were there for three hours. I do not have my calculator but that adds up to about one-eighth of a thousand years and it comes out to something in the neighborhood of a hundred and twenty-five years or so.

This type of reasoning would be demolished by the professional theologians, I know. But the point I am trying to make here is that there is an element of mystery in the pain of Jesus and, really, nobody in his darkest hour and deepest pain can look up to Jesus and say, "You do not know what it is because you have not experienced it." Jesus has experienced it and much more intensely and much more deeply than myself. He does know what it is because He has been there.

In this sense, St. Thomas Aquinas interprets the strange phrase in the Apostle's Creed, "... He descended into hell." In this sense, Jesus descended to the depths of all human suffering and pain, experienced it personally and knows what it is in His heart and in His flesh.

Also, Jesus in His pain and suffering experienced desolation, dryness and depression in His heart and spirit. Without depression there is no real pain. Without desolation and despondency there is no real suffering. So, Jesus suffered not only in His flesh but in the very depths of His soul. And He expresses this in His torment in the garden when He says, "My soul is sorrowful unto death." To paraphrase, "I feel so cut-off and terrible that I would like to die."

Satan attacks Jesus in Gethsemane and on Calvary just as he did in the desert. When we are physically weak and tired, fatigued and in pain, our spirit is most vulnerable and the devil, who is a master of human nature, tries to get us in our weakest, most vulnerable moments. In the desert, he tempts Jesus. He fails and it is written in Scripture, "He left Jesus for a while." This "a while" was three years and he appears again in the garden and he tempts Jesus. Jesus trembles. He is a pitiful sight as he lies there on the ground filled with terror, sweating blood. This is a very strange sight and something difficult to understand. It is an extremely rare medical phenomenon to sweat blood. It occurs in someone who is extremely delicate and sensitive and at the same time who experiences tremendous inner fear and terror. Many men had faced the crucifixion and endured it without this trembling, without this terror, yet there is Jesus, this man of extraordinary courage, looking so weak and pitiful. He is struggling with the devil. He is struggling with this inner despair and tendency to depression. He is struggling with the temptation to give up. This is an important element which one must always bear in mind when considering the suffering of Jesus. It is totally free and consented to from the very beginning to the last moment. In any instant, in any moment, Jesus could have stopped the suffering and the pain.

So, the devil attacks and Jesus fights with him and in His inner agony goes to his friends, Peter, James and John, seeking their support, their sympathy and their understanding. They do not understand his pain and they make it only worse by being indifferent to it and by falling asleep. Here, Jesus gives us an important lesson. If you seek consolation and sympathy and understanding in your pain and suffering from those who are healthy, more likely than not, you will only end up being disappointed. God is my strength. God is my comfort. God is my rock. And as Jesus did, true consolation should be sought and will be found in God and God alone. Jesus continues to struggle with the demons even until the very end. On the cross at Calvary, in this intense pain, He is tempted at all times to come down. If he were not tempted, if he did not feel this inclination to put a stop to the pain and the suffering and torture, he would not have been human. But because His flesh and blood are real, He could not help but experience the desire, the temptation to put a stop to it, to come down from the cross, to put an end to the horrible suffering and to find a release. But He endured it patiently and peacefully, heroically and courageously unto the end. And this is the most outstanding feature of the passion and death of Christ.

Lord Jesus, I think of myself nailed to the cross. I am free to come down. How long would I have freely remained there and endured the pain? I guess it is at most 10 seconds and even then I am being generous and charitable to myself. But, You endured it unto the very end and this is a marvelous expression of your love, your courage, your heroic, extraordinary patience.

Jesus' role on the cross was to pray and to suffer. He offers to the Father His sacrifice of praise, His prayer together with His terrible pain, with His blood. On the cross, He does not preach. He does not teach. He hardly speaks. On the cross, He performs no miracles. He does not heal. He does not visibly help. He does not plan or organize or do anything productive. Yet, on the cross, by His prayer and suffering, Jesus accomplishes the greatest work in the history of mankind. He redeems the world. He sanctifies man. He obtains salvation for us and nothing more noble, exalted or holy can be imagined.

My role, now, is more and more similar to that of Jesus on the cross. My productive hour is over. I can hardly talk. I can no longer preach. I have difficulty in doing anything. So my role is simply to offer my prayer and my pain with Jesus to the Father. And this, I think, will be of more benefit to my children, my sisters, my brothers than all of my brilliant planning and great projects and programs. This is the supreme test and ultimate act of faith and love.

Here, in this chapter, it would be well to advise the reader of what I have concluded to be the will of the Lord concerning the life-support systems of which I wrote in the opening chapter.

My answer is a resounding, " No," at least at this point in time. I feel it would be the height of folly and very presumptuous

of me to go this route. I know myself. I know I have an extremely
low threshold of boredom. I am hyperactive. I am extremely
independent and I have a very limited supply of patience.
Also, apart from the ALS sickness itself, I have many physical weaknesses which are greatly exacerbated by ALS. I won't
bore the reader with a litany of these, but among them is a terrible
digestive system, great sensitivity, a sleeping disorder and severe
arthritis. I truly do not feel that I have the physical stamina nor the
mental stamina and spiritual makeup to lie in bed for an unlimited
number of years, breathing with a tube in my throat and eating
through another tube in my belly and possibly communicating by
blinking my eyelids. I do not see how this would serve any useful
purpose. The people around me are somewhat romantic. They
think I would be an inspiration. Yes, I would be an inspiration if
they saw me all day with a cherubic expression on my face, a sweet
smile on my lips, a bright look in my eyes and always as a perfect
model of patient, heroic courage and quiet determination. But, I
think that image is totally unrealistic. A better image would be
someone terribly frustrated, deeply depressed, looking through
eyes that are glazed and hardly able to communicate. I doubt if I
would be a source of strength to anyone. On the contrary, I might
be a scandal and a stumbling block.

Also, I think of Jesus on the cross. Would the apostles have
been encouraged and strengthened if He remained there forever
without dying? Loving Jesus and knowing Him as a friend, would
they be stimulated and really impelled to do more by thinking of
Him and His pain, and would they draw strength from returning
to the cross and looking up into this face contorted by pain and
suffering? If they were truly friends and their hearts were united
in love, the contrary would be true. So, I don't see where the sisters
and the people about me think they would draw strength from my
lingering in bed, locked into my sickness, nailed to my disease by
this life-support system as the body of Jesus was fixed to the cross
by the nails piercing His hands and His feet.

Also, I do not think I am needed. I feel that this work is the
work of Mary. She is the foundress, the director, the chairman of
the board, the superior and she will see that the work continues to
grow and to flourish. To think that the work will crumble if I

dissolve and disappear is the height of pride, it is a lack of faith and confidence in Mary, Our Mother.

Moreover, if I leave this world, I will not leave the work and the sisters and the children and the brothers. As St. Therese of Lisieux says, "I will come back and continue to do good until the end of the world." Being a hyperactive, restless type, if I go to heaven I will come back and spend my eternity in aiding the sisters and the children in a hidden, secret but very real manner.

Jesus could have remained to assist His apostles by His living, physical presence. But He left them after only three years. They felt very abandoned, frightened, and inadequate to the task that lay ahead of them, but Jesus said, "I leave you for your own good and if you love Me, you will be happy that I am going to the Father." I can make these words my own. If I leave the sisters and the children, I do it for their own good and if they truly love me, they will be happy to see me go to the Father.

But to live is to change. To change often is to be perfect. So I do not categorically eliminate the possibility of changing my mind. But God would have to incline me strongly in that direction. He would have to give me the patience and the courage and the determination beforehand. I cannot pretend to have it and I cannot tempt Him. Jesus in the Gospel says, "If you will build a tower, sit down and calculate. Can you finish it? If not, better not to begin it." The same can be said of someone who sets out to run the full-course marathon which is a little over 26 miles. Can you complete the course? Can you go the distance? If not, better not to begin. And if you're going on a life support system, do you have the will to go, to accept this with calm, serenity, peace and joy and with patience and courage? If the answer is no or very doubtful, best not to go this way. At this point, I do not have the will to go. I cannot complete the course. So it is better, not to go this way, unless the Lord intervenes and makes me see clearly that this is His will and that He will provide the patience, the strength, the courage, the peace which is necessary.

It has so frequently been my experience that I spend a great deal of time rationalizing, drawing up arguments and reasons for one course of action only to find that the Lord leads me in the exact opposite path. So, the man of faith is moved by the Spirit and I invite the Spirit to enter my life, my heart. He's already there and I let myself be moved by the Spirit. So, if the Spirit moves me in this direction of life-support, I will do my best to go in that direction lightly and easily and in a child-like manner.

Many ALS patients who opt for life-support systems are held up as heroes and inspirations. They are praised as determined individuals who do not give up, who cling to life at all cost. This may well be true. But my personal feeling is that many are simply following a basic instinct which is life preservation. They are secretly terrified at the thought of death and hang on to life at any and all cost. Frequently their decision is a very selfish one because it entails enormous sacrifice and suffering for those who must take care of them.

So to conclude this rambling chapter, if it is up to me, the answer to this life-support system, is a clear, solid, resounding, "No." As I write these lines now, I have the conviction that this is the course of prudence and this is what the Lord wants of me.

Chapter 14

Meditation at the Foot of the Cross

T his is a private meditation on Calvary. This chapter is for myself. I imagine that I am standing at the foot of the cross with Mary, her sister, Mary the wife of Clopas, Mary Magdalene, and John, the disciple whom Jesus loved. I look up into the face of Jesus, this man of sorrows, acquainted with grief. He is as a leper, one struck by God, in whom there is neither beauty nor comeliness.

Jesus descended into hell and He came forth victorious, triumphant and glorious. Jesus is the ultimate survivor. He knows the secret of coping with suffering and pain. Not only does he cope with suffering and pain, but he conquers it, he triumphs over it and he turns suffering and pain into something radiant and glorious. What is the secret of Jesus?

ALS is described as a devastating illness, a disease which is very cruel and demeaning. The same can be said of the manner in which Jesus freely chose to die. Death by crucifixion is exceedingly cruel and demeaning.

The Romans were pagans and over the course of a hundred years, they had experimented with the cruelest ways to put a man to death. The result of years of horrible experimentation was the crucifixion. Not only was it excruciatingly painful but it was relatively long and drawn out. More than that, it was extremely debasing, degrading and in every way demeaning. Jesus on the cross was not a figure of glory to be admired. He was stripped naked and held up to the world as a fool and as a laughing stock.

Jesus freely chose this form of death. If He wished, He could have chosen a way to go which was relatively clean and noble. For example, John the Baptist in a secret dungeon had his head severed from his body in one clean stroke and then brought to Herod on a silver platter. Jesus, if He wished, could have chosen this form of execution. He could have had His head separated from His body and offered to the world as an act of redemption on a silver platter. This is relatively quick, clean, noble and non-demeaning. Yet He freely chooses death by crucifixion. He freely chooses the cruelest and most demeaning way to go.

What is extraordinary is the heroic patience, courage and determination which Jesus shows throughout His crucifixion. As has been mentioned in a previous chapter, it is important to bear in mind that Jesus from the very beginning until the very end is perfectly and totally free. He has all the power in heaven and earth and He is in full, complete control of His destiny. At any point during His crucifixion, Jesus could have put an end to the pain, come down from the cross and turned His suffering into joy, pleasure and glory. Yet He not only remains there on the cross, He remains there with utter calm, peace and serenity. He remains there for three hours until the very end. Strictly from the human point of view, this feat of patience and courage is absolutely extraordinary and in every way heroic. The Roman Centurion who witnessed the courage and patience of Jesus and could compare the way He died to that of many other criminals was greatly impressed and so overcome by the example of Jesus that he concluded that such extraordinary patience and courage was more than human. It was superhuman. It was not just natural but supernatural and could come only from God. So he exclaimed, "Truly, was this not the Son of God?"

In the previous chapter, I made the personal observation that if it were I instead of Jesus nailed there to the wood of the cross and I was free to come down, I would have remained there for maybe ten, or at most, twenty seconds before calling it quits. In the Philippines each year on Good Friday, there are men who in their fanaticism or faith, whichever you prefer to call it, have themselves nailed to the cross similar to the manner in which Jesus was nailed. The longest anyone can remain nailed to the cross is about

60 seconds. This is the world record. Yet Jesus remains there for three hours. His name indeed should be recorded in the Guiness Book of World Records. But it was really more than three hours because He is the God-man and there is this theandric element in His suffering. So, He was nailed there more like one hundred twenty-five years than three hours.

What is more, He is not pretending, playacting nor putting on a show on Calvary. It is a great struggle and inner combat that He wages unto the end. He expresses the struggle that goes on in His heart when He mentions in the Garden of Gethsemane, "My God, my God, why have you abandoned Me?" These are not just pious phrases. They reveal the inner depression, despair, despondency and the tremendous battle that was being waged in the heart and soul of Jesus. The devil always exploits our moments of weakness when we are physically weak, tired, exhausted and suffering. When we are most vulnerable, the devil knows and he attacks us the fiercest at these moments. He attacked Jesus in the desert when He was exhausted by His fast and worn out by the silence, boredom and tedium of His stay in the desert. Then the devil went to Gethsemane when Jesus was prostrate on the earth, His face pressed to the ground and sweating blood. The devil was there and covered the hill of Calvary with this darkness, which entered the very depths of the soul of Christ. It was the devil whose voice we hear in the taunts of the onlookers, the priests, the soldiers, the bad thief, the passersby. They shake their heads and cry out, "If you are the son of God, come down from the cross and save yourself." Jesus had to renew His consent to remain there and He struggled from instant to instant and He did this unto the very end.

Some may object that this is pure conjecture and simple pious fantasizing. No, it is based on reality. Jesus was human. He was made of flesh and blood. If He were made of flesh and blood like you and me, He must have experienced these temptations. He must have been greatly tempted to come down from the cross. He must have longed for the release of death. If this were not the case, Jesus was not like us and tempted like us by sin, as St. Paul so clearly states.

I am nailed to the cross of ALS. Each day the struggle

intensifies. The disease is inexorable in its progress. Each day becomes more difficult than the day before, and looking ahead, I see stretching before me uncharted paths of pain, suffering and humiliation. Being a realist, I am trying to find out how to cope, how to survive, more than that, how to overcome, to triumph and to be victorious. The answer is found on Calvary in the person of Jesus. I must aspire to his heroism. I must try to imitate his extraordinary patience and courage, not simply out of supernatural reasons but just out of humanistic concerns. This is the only way to cope and the best way to survive.

First of all, Jesus, who is the Way, the Truth and the Life, speaks of faith, a very mysterious virtue, very difficult indeed to grasp and define. In the Gospel, Jesus says, "In the world you shall have tribulation but take courage, I have overcome the world."

St. Paul, under the inspiration of the Holy Spirit, goes further and he writes, "This is the victory which overcomes the world, our faith."

So faith is the first virtue or quality I must cultivate to cope, survive, overcome and triumph.

By faith, I believe that God chastises those whom He loves. I believe, that, for those whom God loves He makes all things work for their good. I believe that God loves me with an everlasting love. He loves me more than I love myself. He loves me to such an extent that He sends His only Son, Jesus Christ, as a living sacrifice to redeem me. He loves me so much that He sends anew each day His Son, Jesus Christ, as my food and drink in the Eucharist. So, I believe, that ALS is sent to me as a sign of God's love and it is given to me for my own good and happiness. The object of faith is not what is seen but what is not seen. Who can grasp the designs of God? Who can understand His wisdom? "My ways are above your ways, as the heavens are above the earth and my thoughts are different from your thoughts," says the Lord. No, I do not understand with my reason and my intellect why this should be so, but I believe He has sent me ALS as a sign of His love and special favor. I believe this and I try to renew this belief at each instant. So it is, I do not look at ALS as an enemy which I fight. I accept it, embrace it and welcome it as a friend.

I believe in the words of St. Paul that God is faithful and He

118

does not permit us to be tried beyond our strength. With every trial He gives us the strength to endure it and He shows us the way to overcome it. I believe God gives me this pain and suffering. I believe at the same time He gives me the strength and grace to accept it, endure it and cope with it. Jesus says to St. Paul, "My grace is sufficient for you, my strength is made perfect in your weakness." I believe the grace of Jesus will always be adequate. The problem is, I would like it to be more than adequate. But it is enough, just enough, for that moment and that instant. As Jesus on the cross, I do not look back. I do not consider the future but I trust in God. I believe in His grace from instant to instant. Jesus expresses this wisdom of faith in the Gospel when He says, "Do not be concerned about tomorrow. Enough for the day is the evil thereof." Do not be concerned about the next hour, the next moment. Simply believe in God, abandon yourself to Him and trust in Him from moment to moment, instant to instant.

I believe that suffering is redemptive, pain is salvific and death and humiliation are fruitful and productive. St. Paul writes, "Without the shedding of blood, there is no work of salvation." And in a similar manner, Jesus in the Gospel says, "Unless a grain of wheat falls into the ground and dies, it remains alone. If it dies, it bears fruit." So, I believe this suffering, humiliation or pain I endure is purposeful, is fruitful and productive. The blood of Jesus is not enough to redeem the world. This is a strange thing to say but this is God's scheme for redemption and salvation. He has decreed it so. He has designed it thus. He loves us so much He wants us to participate in the greatest, most satisfying and fulfilling work imaginable which is the saving of souls. And, so, He has decreed that all blood must be mingled with the blood of Jesus in order to save and redeem the world. In this spirit, St. Paul writes, "I make up in my body the sufferings which are lacking in the body of Christ."

I believe that in suffering there is already a secret joy and sense of fulfillment which is very subtle, secret and spiritual. In this sense, Jesus in the Gospel says, "Blessed are you who suffer." He uses the present tense. There is a certain secret joy now in suffering and pain. Also, Jesus expresses this when He looks at His approaching passion and death and exclaims. "The time for the glorification of the Son of Man is at hand." And again, St. Paul expresses the same theme when he says, "In the cross of Christ there is salvation, life and resurrection."

Hope is another virtue, very closely related to faith and really difficult to separate and distinguish from faith, which enables us to cope with suffering and be a survivor of the worst pain and humiliation imaginable. By hope we believe in the promise of Jesus and are confident of future reward for any pain and suffering we endure now.

In the Gospel, Jesus speaks of hope to His disciples at the Last Supper. He says, "You will be sad now and weep and wail, but your sadness will be turned to joy and your joy no man will take from you." St. Paul writes on the same theme. He says, "I consider the sufferings of the present moment as nothing when compared to the glory which is to come." And again, St. Paul says, "If we die with Christ, we shall rise with Him and in the measure that we suffer with Him, we will rejoice with Him."

St. Paul writes that "Eye has not seen nor ear heard nor has it so much entered the heart of man the things which God prepares for those whom He loves." In the light of hope, I look beyond the suffering of the present moment and consider it light and a little moment compared to the almost infinite, eternal glory and happiness which lies beyond the suffering and the pain.

Also, in the light of hope, I think of the next world, the real world. This life is like the wrong side of a tapestry. Only in the next life can we see what the design and beauty of the tapestry is all about. In the next world, if I endure suffering for a moment, I will be in the number of those saints and martyrs, who in the words of St. John in the Book of Revelation, have come from the great tribulation. They have washed their robes white and clean in the blood of the Lamb. It is a great thing to have suffered. We have only this brief moment here on earth to experience suffering. Our eternity would be very empty and insipid if we look on this brief moment here on earth and realize we have had an easy, comfortable life. There is a sense of satisfaction, fulfillment and joy from heaven passed through the crucible of suffering and humiliation, the joy of having endured and survived. There is no way that one can experience this vicariously. This pleasure, this joy, this sense of fulfillment was the only thing lacking to the joy of Jesus in heaven. He had everything else in an infinite, eternal degree. So, He came to earth to experience in His own flesh, in His own heart, in His own soul, suffering, pain, humiliation and death. And after passing through these things He said, "Ought not the Son of Man to have suffered all these things in order to enter into His glory?" There was no other way to enter this glory. He could not have had His angels endure this. He had to experience it Himself in order to taste the joy and glory and triumph which lie on the other side.

I ran three full-course marathons when I was in my forties. They were extremely difficult and painful. But there is a general satisfaction in looking back and saying, "I ran the course. I endured it. I lasted until the end." No one who has not experienced this can taste the enormous joy, satisfaction and sense of fulfillment of having experienced this and survived.

So from moment to moment in our pain and suffering, we believe, we hope, we renew acts of faith and hope and we always look away from the pain and suffering and focus our attention on what is positive and good. This is very important.

For example, I am crippled, disabled. I have difficulty breathing, chewing, swallowing, speaking, eating, sleeping, living. I try to turn my attention from these and praise the Lord for what I can do. I can look and see and grasp the beauty of His creation. I can look into the faces of the children, sisters, brothers, the sick who respect and love me and see their smiles and their affection. I can hear music, the sound of the wind and the singing of the birds. I can hear the voices of people who are close to me and who help me. I can think clear thoughts and pray. I can experience the emotional satisfaction of love, affection, respect and friendship. So I try to turn away from the negative, in this spirit of hope, and focus on the positive.

In this spirit, we read in the Psalms, "God rejoices me by all that He does." And, "More than grain and wine, God rejoices my heart." So God gives me suffering and pain, in the words of the Imitation of Christ, "He truly has turned into dust all the consolations ever heard." Yet at the same time He puts into the depths of my heart a new secret joy, a spiritual pleasure and a supernatural peace which surpasses all understanding. So I try to think of these and praise and give glory to God.

Jesus on Calvary, also, teaches us that love is very important in surviving and coping and overcoming. In the Gospel, Jesus says, in reference to his death, "No one takes my life from me. I freely give it in order to take it up again." He freely dies and suffers in order to experience a new life of love. Again, in the Gospel, He says, "If any man renounces his life for my sake, he will find it." You renounce your self to Jesus and die to self by loving, by forgetting yourself, by being indifferent to your self, getting out and away from self and denying self. In doing this you find a new life in God. In this sense, it is written, "Although suffering is in me, I am not in it. I am in God." This is accomplished by love. "Who loves God is in Him and He in them," says St. John the Apostle. So, in suffering I try to overcome my selfishness, forget self, be indifferent to self and love. St. John the Apostle says, "Love casts out all fear. Where there is perfect love, there is no fear." Fear is a symbol of all negative emotions, depression, desolation, sadness, anxiety. The secret to overcome this is love.

Jesus, throughout His passion and death, continues this one unending act of pure, total love. He says, "No greater love has any man than this, that he lay down his life for his friends."

At the last supper and in the garden, when His soul is so depressed He would like to die, He does not succumb to His depression. He does not withdraw into Himself. He continues to love. He thinks of others. He prays for His disciples. He encourages them by His words. He washes their feet. He gives them His flesh and blood as food and drink. In the Garden of Gethsemane, when the soldiers come and take hold of Him to lead Him away to death, Jesus forgets self and thinks of others. He says, "If you seek Me, here I am. Let these go." On the way to Calvary, He falls repeatedly under the weight of His cross, yet He looks at the women who are weeping and expresses His concern for them, "Weep not for Me but for yourselves and your children." And again, on the cross, in His intense pain, He looks at His mother and John and speaks words of comfort and love. "Mother, behold your son. Son, behold your mother." We must remember how difficult it is for Jesus to speak. He can hardly breath. It is so difficult for

Him to get out of His pain, His consciousness is flooded with this sense of pain and suffering. Yet, He continues to love and expresses love by thinking of others and consoling others. He consoles the good thief. He prays for His persecutors.

So in our suffering and pain, it is so easy to become self-absorbed, self-preoccupied, self-conscious. This is the nature of pain and suffering. But we must constantly do our best to look away from it, try to think of others, try to console and comfort others.

In this sense, St. Paul says, "For me to live is Christ, to die is gain." I must die to self. I am nothing. I am of no importance and to live is Christ, Christ in my neighbor, Christ in my brother, Christ in the poor. So I try my best to think of others, to console them, to comfort them, to be kind, to be friendly toward them.

Virtue is its own reward. This is a maxim or an axiom of philosophy or theology. It is so true. If there were no life hereafter and I did not believe in God, the way to survive and overcome suffering and pain is by faith, hope and love. The way to be conquered and defeated is to be without faith, deprived of hope and to be filled with selfishness and preoccupation with self.

There are a few other lessons which I could learn from Calvary. First of all, Jesus suffers in silence. He is as a lamb led away to the slaughter. He does not open His mouth or cry out. In the Gospel, Jesus recommends this kind of suffering. "When you fast," He says, "do not disfigure your face, nor appear to be fasting before men but anoint your head and wash your face. Appear cheerful and happy." This is not simply spiritual guidance but good, solid psychology. By whining and moaning, complaining and groaning, you simply intensify the pain. You multiply the suffering. You increase the difficulty. It is said if you have a thorn in your flesh and you can smile, you are a hero. You are not only a hero but you have discovered the best way of coping with the thorn in your flesh. If you cannot remove it and no one else can, it serves no purpose to constantly shout and scream and talk about it. This only makes it worse. So you try to smile and pretend that it is not there. You try to endure it with silence and patience. This is simply the best way to handle it. On occasion, Jesus did express His pain and suffering but He did it in a very light manner and as

123

a simple, quiet release. He mentions His depression, "I am sorrowful even unto death." He mentions his despair, "Father, why have you abandoned Me?" He mentions His terrible physical pain of dehydration, "I thirst!" But then He does not dwell on these. He passes over them lightly and He presents an attitude of calm, serenity and silence. This is another secret of His suffering which I must try to emulate.

Also, Jesus by example teaches us it is rather futile to seek too much help, comfort and consolation from people. Frequently, they only make things worse. In the Garden of Gethsemane, He goes to His friends Peter, James and John and asks for their support and sympathy. They do not understand His anguish. They are coldly indifferent to it and they simply go to sleep. He seeks consolation from His friends and they only make His suffering and anguish worse. This is frequently our human experience. Suffering is really something which isolates you. It is very difficult for someone else to comprehend and grasp. We can seek counsel and guidance, but, usually, if we complain and explain and talk too much and seek too much consolation from others, we only make things worse. We express our pain to God, as the writers of the psalms do, and we look to God as did Jesus in the Garden of Gethsemane for strength, consolation and joy and comfort.

What I have expressed here is an ideal which Jesus shows us and teaches us in the Gospel and especially on Calvary. It is an ideal which I admire and which I aspire to. My daily reality is quite different. I fall and fail and fumble. This, too, is part of the experience of pain, this experience of our weakness, our powerlessness, our helplessness. If we march through our pain with quiet heroism we will be tempted to pride and self-delusion. So, we aspire to this ideal. We try to cultivate the virtues of faith, hope and love. We do this for Jesus. We do this for supernatural, spiritual reasons. We do it also simply to cope, survive, and eventually to triumph.

Chapter 15

The Summing Up

I am jumping ahead here. I have three or four more chapters which I should complete before winding up this book and writing the final chapter. However, my voice is growing so weak and I seem to be deteriorating so dramatically that I deem it prudent to write this chapter first. Then, afterwards, if I still have enough voice and strength left, I will go back and fill in the chapters which are lacking.

This chapter will be a potpourri, a sort of summing up, a last letter to my daughters, The Sisters of Mary, or, if you will, a spiritual last will and testament. If I were to die after completing this tape, these remarks express what I would like to say to the sisters who remain behind.

First of all, I wish to repeat no matter how critical my physical condition becomes, under no circumstances do I wish to go on life support and be hooked up to a ventilator, thus being permanently locked into my disease. I urge those who are taking care of me to resort to no extraordinary means to prolong my life. I ask, if at some point in my illness I stop breathing and go into respiratory arrest, that you do not try to revive me by artificial respiration. If you want to give me a kiss, place your sweet lips on my forehead, give me your kiss of peace and send me home to my Father, lightly, easily and in a trusting, child-like manner.

Please do not interpret this decision as a cowardly one. I think in making such a decision, I am following the example of Jesus.

He left His disciples on their own after just three short years of training and preparation. They were panic stricken at the thought of His departure. They were convinced they were not ready and they would never make it on their own. Yet, Jesus, by choice goes to Jerusalem and deliberately gives Himself up to death. He could have very easily survived and remained with His disciples not for three years but for another thirty years if He chose to do so.

However, in His wisdom He knew that they would grow and mature spiritually without Him. Also, once He was nailed to the cross, Jesus went very quickly. Some criminals remained nailed to their crosses for as long as two or three days without expiring. The other two who were nailed to the cross with Jesus were still alive, but after just three hours Jesus had already expired.

It is possible, if there had been modern medical facilities at that time, that Jesus could have been kept alive on the cross for a considerably longer period of time. He died of suffocation. If a tracheostomy had been performed and He was hooked up to a respirator, if He were given copious blood transfusions and certain pain killers and stimulants, it is very possible that He could have been kept on the cross alive for several more days. This would have been terribly cruel. It would have been an act of barbarism. Jesus did not want to prolong His stay, so, He went very cleanly and quickly.

Also, at the Last Supper, Jesus looked at His friends and He was filled with love and compassion. "You have been with Me from the beginning of my tribulation," says Jesus. I can say this to you, my daughters, also. You have suffered with me, endured many trials and survived much combat. So, there is not only this bond of faith which unites our hearts, but, there is also the bond of common suffering, battle and tribulation. So our hearts are really one in Jesus. Yet Jesus says to His disciples, "If you love me you will be happy that I am going to my Father." And again, "I go to my Father because it is for your good." Finally He says, "I will come back. I will be with you all days even unto the end of the world and I will not leave you orphans."

I hope it is not pretentious nor too bold if I speak similar words. If you truly love me, you will be happy that I go to the Father. In fact, now you should pray that I go quickly and that God grant me the grace of a happy, holy, peaceful death. And pray that I go directly to heaven without any detour to that mysterious and troubling place called purgatory. Also, be convinced, if I go it will redound to your own good and for the good of our work. You will be amazed that you will do much better without me. You will grow, develop and mature in the Lord. In the words of St. Paul, "The power of Jesus in you can do infinitely more than you dream of, think of, or imagine."

Also, being the hyperactive type, if I go to the Lord I do not plan to stay put in heaven, clothed in white, with a palm branch in my hand spending my days singing the praises of the Lord before the throne of the Lamb. I hope to come back and assist you in every way. I can help you more, at this point, in heaven than here on earth.

Also, to pursue this theme further, imagine Mary who loves her son, Jesus, more than herself, standing at the foot of the cross in the darkness. She looks up at the disfigured face of Jesus. She is very sensitive. She feels in every fiber of her being, to the very core of her soul, the terrible pain, suffering and agony which Jesus is enduring. What do you think was the theme of her prayer during the three hours at the foot of the cross on calvary?

I do not think she prayed, "Father do not let Him die. Keep Him there on the cross for as long as possible, another two or three days, or at least two or three hours. I do not want Him to close His eyes and pass into death." I do not think this would have been a prayer of love. I think she would have prayed with the compassion of a mother's heart, "Father, have pity on his suffering. Look at his pain, is it not enough? Please put an end to it quickly. Grant him release and call him to your eternal peace and glory." I recommend that you have similar sentiments in your heart and that you try praying in a like manner.

Now let me change the subject to another important matter, namely, formal recognition and the approval on the part of Rome of the Sisters of Mary. Do not be overly concerned or expend a great deal of mental energy on this point.

With many misgivings and a great deal of reluctance, I have

done my best to prepare the many documents required to obtain formal approval from Rome. I did this mostly at the insistence of Cardinal Sin. Also, I feel that it might be beneficial to the charity programs of the Sisters of Mary, after I am gone. But I have mixed feelings on this point.

The Sisters of Mary were founded in 1964. For nearly thirty years now, we have not only survived without formal approval from Rome but we have grown, prospered and flourished to a remarkable degree. We have no internal problems to speak of. The children each day grow in wisdom, age and grace before the Lord. The morale of the sisters is soaring. We have no financial problems, thanks be to God. So, I am not convinced that approval or recognition from Rome will add anything significant in the way of better results or more spiritual fruits. If suddenly we got a document with the stamp of approval from Rome, it would not bring in more candidates to the sisters, it would not generate more funds, it would not, in any way, help the children study better or achieve better success. Permission from Rome might merely serve to complicate our style and thwart many of our efforts to serve the poor.

In all good faith and with tremendous effort, especially at this time in my life when I have so many other things to be concerned with, I did my best and on two occasions I prepared, assembled and sent, through Cardinal Sin, copious documents to Rome. Rome seems to have an insatiable appetite for paper, for the written word, for documents. Their motto seems to be, "By their documents you shall know them." The more documents we send the more they ask for and demand. Their approach seems so cold, impersonal, bureaucratic and legalistic that I find it repugnant and very much in the spirit of the Pharisees at the time of Christ.

Those in Rome do not seem to be concerned with the good of the poor, achieving results and doing something positive and constructive. They seem more concerned with principles of authority, with dead laws and written rules and regulations.

But do not be concerned if Rome hesitates to grant us formal approval or recognition. It will come in time. The important thing is that this work is approved and recognized by the powers of heaven. There is no doubt, whatsoever, that the spirit of the Lord hovers over these programs and dwells in our midst, directs and moves us. Unless the spirit of the Lord were in us and with us, this spirit of charity, these works in no way would be possible.

At the time of Christ the Pharisees would not accept His words, His statements, His powerful message. So He said, "If you do not believe my words, look at my works and believe them." The logic behind this statement is, if God were not with us, these marvelous works of charity and marvels of service could not happen.

God has for thirty years performed works of charity, marvels of service, and miracles of mercy through us, in us and with us, and these miracles continue each day, despite a million obstacles and constant attacks from so many enemies from about, including officials of the church and the government. This work is so obviously of God that there should be no doubt or question on this score. So the important thing is, we have the approval and recognition from God. If the church withholds its approval, we accept this simply and it is good because it keeps us humble.

Also, think of the story of the Good Samaritan. In the Gospel, Jesus uses this person as a model of service and a hero of charity and mercy. Yet he was treated as an outcast and a heretic by the authorities of the church of that day and age. Those that were recognized by the church, namely the priest and the deacon, did nothing for the man who was naked and bleeding and dying by the side of the road. At least in Korea, the Sisters of Mary have been treated as outcasts, heretics, rejects or pariahs for more than twenty years. But this in no way should be a source of concern or should it disturb us.

We have drawn up and submitted constitutions in which we have made many compromises with the bureaucratic, authoritarian, legalistic spirit of Rome. I have done this very reluctantly, but, remember, even if these constitutions are approved, the basic law and that which supersedes all else is the law of charity, the law of mercy and service. The letter of the law kills but the spirit of the law gives life. The spirit of the law of God and the spirit of our constitutions is charity. "Above all else," says Saint Paul, "have charity." So every rule and regulation which may be formally approved must always be interpreted in the light of charity.

If in any way to serve that rule prevents us from serving the poor and instead of helping, hinders us in the practice of charity, then, we discard the lesser rule and regulation which is written on paper and opt for this higher rule of charity which comes from God. Let me give but one example. Rome says that the novitiate be apart from the regular community, that novices do not engage in the everyday liberties of a religious group, but for a year or two they live a life apart. There is no way we could keep this rule without sacrificing many children and without hurting our work. We simply do not have enough personnel to take ten or fifteen novices and send them to a quiet place for a year or two where they tend the garden, practice needlepoint, play and study. Not only that, but they would come forth from this spiritual desert of a withdrawn novitiate less prepared for the calling of active service and charity which is theirs. So, even if the constitutions approved by Rome say the opposite, the law of charity dictates that we lightly and easily ignore this type of defying regulation. Why then go through with the rigmarole of obtaining approval, if we do not intend to observe the rules and regulations approved? Does this not smack of duplicity and hypocrisy? St. Dominic uses the phrase, "holy hypocrisy." In a sense we could call what we are doing holy hypocrisy. It might be a little duplicitas but if it is for the good of the children, the sick and the suffering then it takes on the aspect of something good and desirable.

This sounds like Jesuitry. The Jesuits were accused of being cute and overly clever, duplicitas, devious and hypocritical. Unfortunately, many authorities in Rome seem to force one to take this path.

Whether Rome approves or not, rest assured that God is with us. If God is with us who can be against us? Mary is with us. If she is with us who can be against us? So I trust this work to Mary. She will remain as director, chairman of the board, founder, helper, protector and friend. Cast all your cares upon the Lord and He will sustain you. So you should entrust all your concerns and cares about the future to Jesus and His Mother, Mary. Go forth with confidence, joy and lighthearted trust.

Another matter which I would like to address in this final chapter is that of succession. For years people have been asking me the questions, "What happens when you die? What happens when you are no longer around? Who will succeed you? Who will continue your work?"

Nothing will change essentially after I am gone. In a sense, it will be business as usual. What do I mean by this?

The real Director and Chairman of the Board of the Sisters of Mary is Mary, Our Lady of Banneux, the Virgin of the Poor. As a Sister of Mary, if you do not believe this basic fact, you do not truly believe in the Sisters of Mary. As for myself, I am utterly convinced of its reality.

By an absolutely unusual set of circumstances, I was ordained a deacon for the diocese of Liege, Belgium in which is located the village of Banneux. Not only that but I was ordained by Bishop Louie Joseph Kerkhofs who was the same Bishop presiding at the time of the apparitions. My priesthood belongs to the Virgin of the Poor. My apostolate has been dedicated to her and from the very beginning, the Sisters of Mary and I have been in her capable, maternal hands.

If this were not so, the sisters would never have come into existence. If this were not so, after the Sisters of Mary were founded, they would never have survived the many trials and tribulations that assailed them. What is more, if Mary were not with us in a very real, active way, the sisters would not have grown, prospered and flourished in the remarkable way which they have done.

Mary will continue to be with the sisters. She will guide, direct, rule, supervise, help them, bless and fructify their work. So really, there is no reason to be concerned over the matter of succession.

But grace works with nature, is founded on nature and perfects nature. So, I realize we must do our best to cooperate with the grace from the Virgin of the Poor, and do our best to make plans and organize. I would like my successor to be one of the sisters. I would like her to be vested with the same power and authority which I have enjoyed over the years. Outsiders, on occasion, have mistaken my style of government or leadership. Some have called it a one-man show. Others have accused me of being a benign dictator. This is not at all accurate.

Every decision I have ever made concerning the Sisters of Mary has always been in close consultation, dialogue and discussion with all the sisters, from the youngest to the oldest. Everyone makes their contribution. Everyone adds their input. I put more importance, of course, on the opinions of those who are entrusted with positions of responsibility. After receiving input from all the members, I make the decision and we move ahead.

This very simple, clean, uncomplicated style of leadership has been most effective and most efficient. By their fruits you shall know them. This style of leadership works and produces fruits in an amazing manner. For example, I know of few religious groups or communities who could go to a completely unknown country like Mexico and within a period of eighteen months purchase land, set up a corporation, recruit Mexican candidates, build three major Boystown/Girlstown buildings, start on a second phase of construction, round up nearly a thousand deprived children, hire teachers and get started. It would take most groups years to discuss and to approve at various levels every decision involved here. They would spend weeks, months and years having meetings before they would proceed with an undertaking of this magnitude. The Sisters of Mary have been able to move so quickly and act so dynamically because of the very open, free-wheeling style of leadership and management. It works so why change it. I would like to see it continue in my successor.

I personally name, Sister Michaela Kim, as the one to succeed me. She will have all authority concerning finances, personnel, expansion, construction and anything else major or minor. In a word, she will be looked upon as my alter ego although I am no longer here. She will decide on every matter in the same way that I have always decided, namely in dialogue and discussion with all the other sisters, especially those in positions of authority.

After I am gone, this form of government should be tried for a period of six years or so. Then the sisters, who have been in vows for a period of ten years, will get together and with the Holy Spirit they will decide if it is good for them or not. If it is good they will continue in this manner. If not, it can be changed or modified as seems proper and fitting.

Sister Michaela, I think, is the natural choice. Our ecclesiastical protector is Cardinal Sin. Our headquarters is in Manila and this is where Sister Michaela has her base of operations. Also, since the Sisters of Mary are now international, it is important to have someone with international experience and a command of English. It is equally important to have one person who can represent the Sisters of Mary and speak for them as a group to the directors of our fund-raising operations in various countries, especially Germany, Switzerland, Austria, Holland and the United States.

Also, in this chapter, I would like to say a word or two about the allocation of money. The Sisters of Mary are a dynamic group. We have, from our very inception, always been expanding, developing and growing. Since our inception in 1964, I cannot recall a period of time during which we did not have some construction underway or we were not planning some form of expansion. It has been a very high-risk venture. Initially, we had very little money and every new project entailed enormous risks. But God has blest this spirit richly and abundantly. The more risk we took and the more we expanded, the more did the money come in. And that has been the pattern from the very beginning.

With regards to finances, we should establish a happy balance between blind, total trust and the providence of God and hard-headed planning and investing for the future. I suggest we try to accumulate a fund for each country which will assure the maintenance of the programs in that country for a period of two or three years, if all outside funds were suddenly to disappear.

After this money has accumulated, it is a sign to expand and develop. Accumulating too much money can destroy the program. It can suffocate it by its materialism. It can make it bloated, fat, lazy and unproductive. Worse than not having enough money is having too much money.

After we accumulate sufficient funds for investments and savings, our first area of development should be Mexico. The Chalco property can easily accommodate between five to seven thousand children. My suggestion is to build two buildings for the boys and on the lower part of the property four buildings for the girls. This means you can accommodate about 2,400 boys and approximately 4,800 girls.

In the Philippines, we should continue our search for another tract of land in the Cebu area preferably in Talisay of five to ten hectares. After we have graduated two or three groups of children from our Cebu Boystown and Girlstown and have the necessary experience, we should replicate what we have done in the Manila area, namely, separate the boys and the girls. We would have one complex in Cebu for girls and another for boys. In total, if we were to do this, the Cebu program would match in numbers what we have in the Manila area, namely six to seven thousand children.

Demographers estimate that the population of the Philippines will have doubled in thirty years time. It is obvious, then, that the need for our program will be all the more acute. The Philippines is a marvelous area of opportunity and a natural place for continuing expansion.

Then in Mexico, after completing construction of the Chalco complex, the possibility of duplicating this program in Guadalajara should be studied. If it seems feasible, land can be purchased there and a program similar in scope can be set up. The population of Mexico now stands at about eighty-five million. This too is predicted to double in about thirty or forty years time. So, the need in Mexico is equally as great and pressing as in the Philippines.

After developing the programs fully in the Philippines and Mexico, then I would suggest looking at the possibility of moving to a fourth country. My first choice would be Brazil which is the largest country in South America, the poorest and perhaps the neediest in terms of spiritual, apostolic considerations.

All of this of course is very risky. It is possible that many of our fund-raising operations might hit hard times. There might be recessions or depressions or other problems and the funds may dry up. But in due time we should develop fund-raising operations within each country where we have established our programs. Already we are doing this in Korea and are amazed at how much money is coming in from within the country. In time our graduates in the Philippines will generate a great deal of income to help our programs. Mexico is also another area where there are many rich people, rich companies and also with many graduates, money will come from within the country itself.

So, the Sisters of Mary are always dynamic, moving, expanding. They have blind confidence in God, yet they proceed with hard-headed, realistic sense and common sense, good investment and good planning. There is always this combination, this balance, nothing excessive. Excessive confidence and trust is presumptuous. Excessive investment and planning is proud and a sign of a lack of faith. There should always be this happy, blessed balance which is arrived at by consultation with the spirit of the Lord, by reading the signs, by much reflection, discussion, patient waiting, experience and intuition.

One final subject which I should treat is that of sainthood. Somehow the word sticks in my throat. I choke on it.

I am even afraid to write about it, but so many people close to me and far removed have been saying such extravagant things and seem to expect such extravagant things, that, at the same time, I am amazed, flattered and heavily burdened.

If anyone speaks of me as a saint, it means one of two things. Either he does not know what a true saint is or else he does not know what I am. The true saint is one who has the habit of extraordinary, heroic virtue. I do not fit this description, believe me.

I must admit when I was young and foolish I dreamed of becoming a saint, similar to John Bosco, St. Vincent de Paul, John of God, Elizabeth Ann Seton or Mother Frances Cabrini. This ALS sickness, however, has really ground me to powder. I have experienced, to a degree difficult to express, my weakness and frailty. I have no illusions, whatsoever, about being a saint.

If there is any goodness or virtue in me, I attribute it totally to the prayers of Sister Gertrude, who spent over thirty years praying for me. She died just six months ago and she continues to watch and pray for me in Heaven. I attribute it to all my Sisters of Mary, my Brothers in Christ, sons and daughters and all my other friends. I attribute it to the blood of Christ.

However, the idea of having an official title of "Saint" before my name for all eternity, to wear a halo, to wear the white garment and carry the palm branch of victory and spend an eternity in the ranks of true, great saints fills me with horror, loathing and even disgust. If forced to do this, by some quirk of faith or design of

God, I would spend my eternity feeling like a phoney, a hypocrite, or a play actor. Truly I do not want this.

However, if the sisters and the children want a Saint as a founder, and I think it would be a great source of encouragement and grace to have one, I put the burden on them. In order to be canonized the Church demands miracles, but, remember the greatest miracle is the miracle of charity — love.

If, after I am gone, the sisters continue to practice love of God by being faithful to their three hours of prayer in union with Jesus on the Cross, if they practice charity toward their neighbor by brotherly love in a model manner, and if they practice charity toward the poor by serving them in the name of Christ in an exemplary fashion, this will be greater than all the miracles of nature, healing or the material kind. The authorities in the Church will look at this miracle of charity and conclude somehow that I am responsible, although I am not, and this will be a strong argument for — God forgive me for even mentioning it — sainthood or canonization.

Usually one or two miracles of nature are also required, miracles of healing. But with so many sisters and children praying and so many hospitals and medical programs under our care, the sisters should be able to document one, two, three or more unexplained healings, for they frequently occur. The church can then decide if they meet the necessary requirements to be recognized as a miracle.

To conclude then, if you want a saint for a founder you assume the responsibility. As far as I am concerned, it would be placing another heavy burden on me, but, if you and the Lord want it, I am willing, although very, very reluctant to accept it and live with it for all eternity.

Chapter 16

Sister Saint Gertrude

A s a professional writer, I am a hopeless case. This chapter should have been completed in the early stages of this book. I am not sure I can complete this chapter because my voice is almost inaudible and my pronunciation is becoming more and more unintelligible. This chapter should not be viewed as an unimportant postscript or epilogue. It is not simply something tacked on to the rest of the book as an afterthought.

This chapter is at the heart and center of this story. In fact, it is the cornerstone of the edifice of my life. If there is any goodness or virtue in me, I attribute it to the prayers and penances of Sister Gertrude, who is the subject of this chapter. If there are any accomplishments and fruitfulness in my life, I think it is due to Sister Gertrude.

Let me explain how God is a God of encounters. He arranges the meeting of certain souls for their mutual benefit and for His glory and the good of the Church. This God of encounters, at a very early stage in my priestly life, arranged for my meeting of Sister Gertrude of the Carmel of Pusan. Sister Gertrude, in turn, was moved by the spirit of God to adopt me as her spiritual or mystical brother. This, of course, is part and parcel of the mission of a Carmelite to convert sinners and pray for priests, especially missionaries.

For more than thirty years hidden in the desert of a Korean Carmel, like the holy prophetess Anna in the Gospel of St. Luke, Sister Gertrude prayed for me and my many projects and fasted and sacrificed and did penance day and night. Unless the grain of wheat falls into the ground, it will not bear fruit. The grain of wheat is the life of Sister Gertrude. The food is the visible works and accomplishments in my priestly life.

In the course of my life on earth, I have met many good, pious, and holy people. In an earlier chapter, I spoke of Sister Vincent as one of these people. If you were to rate holiness on a scale of one to ten, I would put the great saints, like John of the Cross, Catherine of Siena, and the Cure D'Ars, these superstars or world-class spiritual champions, in the nine and ten category. I would give little Sister Vincent of the Sisters of Mary, a four. Sister Gertrude, I would rate much higher, I would give her a seven or maybe an eight.

Sister Gertrude is another person I consider canonizable. However, she has certain disadvantages from a strictly human point of view. It would help enormously in the process of canonization to die young, preferably under the age of thirty five, to have a very pretty face and to live in a Carmel geographically close to Rome. Unfortunately, Sister Gertrude died at the age of ninety three. Although, from a spiritual point of view, her face was radiant, youthful, and very attractive, from a physical point of view, she can only be charitably described as homely. Also, she spent the last thirty or more years of her life in an obscure Carmelite convent in Korea. What is more, the Korean sisters who remain behind at this Carmel have neither the political power nor the financial power to pursue successfully her cause of canonization. She most likely will never be canonized. However, as an unofficial committee of one, I declare her a saint and in this chapter, I will refer to her as Sister Saint Gertrude.

I made her acquaintance shortly after I arrived in Korea in 1957. I visited the Carmel of Pusan on Christmas day. I went there to see an American Carmelite from Washington, D.C. whom I had known prior to my arrival in Korea. During my visit I was introduced to Sister Saint Gertrude. She was almost twice my age. I was about thirty and she was sixty or more. It is interesting to note that Saint Theresa of Avila was twice the age of Saint John of the Cross when they first encountered each other.

Sister Saint Gertrude was a native of Belgium, the daughter

of an aristocratic family. She entered the Carmel in Belgium and served two terms as Prioress before volunteering to go to the newly established convent of Pusan, Korea.

Sister Saint Gertrude's beginnings in Korea were most difficult. She arrived in 1955 at the very inception of the Carmel. The house was poorly heated, the food was inadequate, but more than anything else, there were tremendous internal problems. What is more, Sister Saint Gertrude knew no Korean and she could communicate in French with just one sister and in English with the American Carmelite, who had a very difficult temperament. After a year or two, she gave up and returned to Belgium. In the home country, she had a change of heart and asked to be given a second chance. She returned to Pusan in 1958 and remained there until her death in 1991.

I became aware of the spiritual power of Sister Saint Gertrude in 1962. Bishop Choi had received a letter from Cardinal Agagianian, Prefect of the Sacred Congregation of the Propagation of the Faith in Rome. The Cardinal had received complaints from American bishops about the fund-raising activities, which I was directing under the auspices of Bishop Choi in the United States. Cardinal Agagianian ordered Bishop Choi to stop his fund-raising activities. We, of course, did not stop and Rome, a month or two later, sent a sharply worded telegram telling Bishop Choi to cease and desist immediately, if not sooner.

After conferring with Bishop Choi, it was decided that I should go to Rome to plead our cause. I had mixed feelings about undertaking this impossible mission. On one hand, I would have been relieved to see Korean Relief or Asian Relief as it was later called, disappear. I was not too excited about fund-raising and I felt this might be a heavy burden on my priesthood. Still at the same time there was an impulse in me which urged me to do my best to keep it going. Before leaving for Rome, I paid a visit to Sister Saint Gertrude and asked for her spiritual support.

I could write a book about my impossible mission to Rome. I felt like I was walking a tightrope which stretched from Korea to the Holy City, to the U.S. and then back to Korea and there was no safety net under the tightrope. I went to Rome. I pleaded our case during an unforgettable interview with Cardinal Agagianian. He was supportive and agreed to close his eyes to our activity in the U.S. Also, as a souvenir of my visit, he gave me a huge ciborium. It was so big, it reminded me of the Wimbledon Cup. So, I returned to Pusan in triumph, holding the ciborium above my head in two hands and presenting it to a chuckling and gleeful Bishop Choi.

My trip to Rome was not a simple quick visit. It involved a great deal of preparation, international phone calls, written reports, planning and maneuvering. At every step of the way, I was at risk, one false move and everything would have been lost. However, I felt I was being guided by a clear wisdom and I was being helped by an invisible power. When I returned to Pusan, Sister Saint Gertrude told me she had been praying for the success of my mission, day and night. So, she was the one who achieved this first victory.

I made many visits to the Carmel of Pusan. I became a close friend of Sister Saint Gertrude but strictly on the spiritual level. From a human point of view, I did not find her very attractive nor appealing. However, she probably felt the same way towards me. However, there was this spiritual faith which united us in our hearts. We were one in Jesus.

We had many differences over the years. She was greatly disappointed in her protege because he showed very little interest in the Second Vatican Council. Sister Saint Gertrude, however, felt this was the greatest event since the coming of the Holy Spirit at Pentecost.

I was in Rome to meet Bishop Choi during the council. Bishop Choi wanted me to attend one or two sessions of this historical gathering. I declined and went on to the United States to take care of my business. Looking back, I think the Second Vatican Council can be called a fair council. Yes, the Holy Spirit was at work and it was infallible, but judging by the standard of Christ: by their fruits you shall know them. Looking at the fruits of the Second Vatican Council, it can only be described as a failure. I still feel little enthusiasm for the beautiful and inspiring documents which were issued from the historical ecclesiastical gathering.

After a while, Sister Saint Gertrude suggested that I not visit the Carmel personally. She feared it took up too much of my valuable time. She suggested that I write letters. By and large, I followed her advice and would write her frequently without any restraint about what was in my heart.

Later I learned that she shared my very personal communiques with her fellow Carmelites. In so doing, she secured the spiritual involvement and support of the entire community for my works and programs.

When I wrote sister of my decision to go the Philippines, she thought I was making a major blunder. Later, she wrote to apologize and asked me to excuse her timidity and lack of trust. Also, she was not enthusiastic about the involvement of the Sisters of Mary in Pro-life, anti-abortion activity. Later, however, she realized again very humbly, that her original reaction was mistaken.

About twenty years before her actual death, she wrote that she had a medical problem which could cause her death at any moment. She was in her early seventies at that time. She expressed a strong desire to leave this vale of tears, to go to her eternal reward in heaven. She asked that I pray that the Lord would call her quickly. Life at Carmel of Pusan had improved considerably but it was still not easy. She never really learned Korean. It is a language too difficult to learn when you are past sixty. So she lived not only the life of a contemplative but really that of a hermit and recluse as well.

I forgot to mention that I offended her and her fellow Carmelites previously when I wrote about them indirectly in my book, "The Starved and The Silent" published by Doubleday in 1966. I unfavorably compared the ease and comfort of their style of life to that of their Buddhist counterparts in Korea which was much more austere, poor and ascetic.

Objectively, their life was very difficult and certainly poor enough but I wrote these lines in a Korea which was destitute and I wrote them from an idealism which could have been mistaken at that time. I felt what I wrote was justified. Now thirty year later, I certainly would not write in the same way. However, even those who share a common faith at the same level, have disagreements and different ways of looking at the same things.

God, in his wisdom, did not choose to call Sister Saint Gertrude to Himself as quickly as she desired. Later, she wrote me that the greatest cross in her life was old age. Her physical strength was failing her. She could not communicate with those about her and life at most had been extremely difficult for her.

The last two or three years of her life were years of great suffering and pain. During the final six months, she was totally paralyzed, could hardly speak and was suffering from cancer of the breast. She showed remarkable patience and courage. I used to visit her frequently when she was an invalid. The sisters arranged for me to enter the Carmel. My passport into the enclosure was a stole. They had me hear her confession as an excuse to see her or else administer the Sacrament of the Sick, although she had received it many times beforehand.

Sister Saint Gertrude was greatly affected by the news of my terminal illness called ALS. She devoted more and more of her prayers and her sacrifices for me and especially my new undertaking in Mexico.

Finally, she died in April of 1990. I was in Mexico at the time. The hour of her death was four in the afternoon Korean time, which was midnight in Mexico. About midnight, I was awakened by the sound of our two dogs barking very excitedly and vociferously. The barking continued for at least an hour. This was not the first time this had occurred but this was the first time they had barked with such excitement for so long. I was wondering what was going on outside when I looked up from my bed to see Sister Cecille who had entered my room and was standing looking out the window. Sister Cecille had never done this before. She never entered during the night without being summoned. I asked her what the problem was. She said something seemed very strange because the dogs were so agitated and excited and after a while she laughed.

The next morning at breakfast, I received a call from Sister Sophia in Pusan. Immediately, I knew the news and the purpose of the call. Yes, Sister Saint Gertrude had died. I felt she stopped by Mexico to say goodbye on her way to the Lord.

Sister Saint Gertrude spent the last years of her life praying and interceding for me before the Lord. She continues this same activity in heaven. I am very grateful for this friend and I trust in the power of her prayer before the throne of the Lord to receive the grace of patience, peace and a happy and holy death.

Chapter 17

Medical Update

I am not sure but I think I might have one chapter left in my failing voice. If I do this will be it.

First of all a medical update may be in order. If memory serves me right I spoke of the trials and tribulations of an ALS victim way back in July or August, 1991. In fact, I detailed a more or less typical day in my life. Now it is March, 1992 and it is a completely different ball game.

If the going was tough in July, well, right now it is much tougher. Truly I underestimated this disease. I have read accounts of other ALS victims in which the disease was called hideous and devastating. I concur with these descriptions. All pain and suffering is both objective and subjective. Objectively, two people can experience the same illness but because of a tremendous difference in sensitivity the pain index can vary enormously. I have always been extremely sensitive. Also, my constitution has always been physically weak and sickly. So, it is not so much the ALS, but, my many other ailments, which are now greatly exacerbated by the ALS which makes the going all the more difficult. Also, temperamentally I am very active, independent and private. ALS robs you of all privacy and independence and renders you totally passive.

I compare the course of ALS to running a twenty-six mile-plus marathon which I did in my forties on at least three occasions. The final five miles are the toughest. In July I was beginning the last five miles, so the going was already getting tough. But of the last five miles, the last mile or so is pure torture and undiluted torment. I am now into my last mile or I certainly hope so. The goal line is in view but it is increasingly difficult and painful.

Dr. Norris, my medical expert, guesses that at most I have another month or two left. ALS is unpredictable so it could be less or it could be more. But all things being equal, I am close to the end. Let me try to describe a typical day in my life at this stage of the illness.

At 5:10 in the morning, the two Sisters who care for me enter my room. They get me out of bed and into my wheelchair. My mouth is so dry that I can hardly speak an intelligible sound. Sister gives me a glass of orange juice. I can still get it down but it is difficult. There is a great deal of gurgling and strange sounds in my throat. This is followed by a little coffee which I sip with a straw.

As Sister is shaving me I look at the day that stretches before me. There is a sinking feeling and I ask myself how can I make it through this day. Then, I reject this thought and try to focus on the present moment. I must live not from day to day or even hour to hour but simply from minute to minute trusting in God, constantly speaking the name of Jesus and Mary, not to be holy or perfect, but simply to survive and keep from getting terribly depressed, despondent and frustrated.

I am vested with the Mass garments and then wheeled to the chapel. I have a frontal headache due to a lack of oxygen. My guess is that my breathing is somewhere in the twenty to thirty percent range of normal. Also, due to the lack of oxygen and the buildup of carbon dioxide, I am overcome with great sleepiness that is close to a light coma. At times I am afraid I will fall ignominiously out of my wheelchair and land at the feet of the Sisters with an unedifying, dramatic bang.

The Sisters play one of my previous meditations on the tape recorder. I listen to my voice and I am amazed that I sounded so good such a short time ago. I am grateful for these meditations. They are simply the Gospel, but, somehow they are a source of life and strength to me in my present condition.

At the end of the meditation, Sister will give me a drink of water and I am placed in front of the altar for Mass. Mass is physically and psychologically a very painful experience. It is so painful to speak and I look at the gospel of the day and groan inwardly if it is a lengthy one. Also, at Mass, I am struggling to keep my head erect and to avoid having it fall down on my chest. If it does someone will have to come to my rescue and lift it up again. Also, at Communion when Brother Tony gives me the host and just a little of the Precious Blood I must be careful not to choke and gag.

After Mass, I am brought to my room. The Sisters help get me on the exercise bike. They strap my arms to the handles with velcro and I somehow move the pedals for fifteen or twenty minutes. The Sisters are experts in handling me, but, I must admit, I make things easy for them because I have lost so much weight. I am not sure what I weigh right now, but, my guess is that it is somewhere between 100 and 110 pounds. I always prided myself on being a fearless realist. I wanted the facts no matter how painful. But, I really don't want to know how much I weigh. I am afraid at this point it might be demoralizing. Besides, I don't know any way that I can weigh myself without endangering my faltering life and my weakened limbs.

After the bike riding, the Sisters do some range-of-motion therapy with my arms and hands. Then I work out a little on what is called an Intermittent Positive Pressure Breather. This is a machine which while not prolonging your life will help expand the lungs and make things a little more comfortable. To date I have seen no positive results from the machine, but I do what I can and go through the motions for five minutes or so.

Next comes breakfast. This is not only burdensome but downright painful. My neck and shoulders are in pain as I try to get in the proper position to swallow without choking. It is very difficult to chew and more difficult to swallow.

After breakfast, Sister will leave me with a cup of coffee with a straw right at the edge of my lips, and I will look out the window sipping coffee and trying to plan how to use to best advantage the day which stretches before me.

I call Sister on the intercom and she returns about quarter to nine. She gives me a subcutaneous injection of morphine. This was strongly recommended by my physician. He assures me there is

no danger, whatsoever, of addiction or even developing toler-
ance. It also helps with the swallowing and it makes me more
relaxed and less uncomfortable. I take the minimal dosage recommended. In fact, I take only half of what was prescribed. I will take
one injection at breakfast, another at noon and another in the
evening. Depending on the level of discomfort or pain I will
increase or decrease the amount.

After I get my morning fix, Sister puts me in a reclining chair
which is well padded and cushioned. Despite the morphine
injection there is always discomfort or pain. All day long I have
trouble with the secretions in my mouth. They cause me to choke
or cough or gag. They are a steady drip, drip, drip similar to
Chinese water torture which can be extremely annoying. Also, I
am so thin, now, all my bones protrude. They cause a lot of
discomfort and pain. Even sitting is painful. Lying in bed my heels
hurt because of the pressure on the bed. My spine and shoulder
blades also hurt. The morphine makes this more or less tolerable.
However, it is difficult to do any creative, productive work
because of the lack of a voice and because of the great drowsiness
and sleepiness and fatigue due to the oxygen shortage. At times
there is a great deal of trembling or fasciculating in my legs and
torso. This can be very painful. I take medication which more or
less helps to control this.

I rest in my easy chair, which is really not all that easy
anymore, for an hour or so. Then I change to the wheelchair. I have
a voice amplifier which is attached to my head. The microphone
is right next to my lips. I will have a meeting with the Sisters to
discuss construction in Cebu, the problems in Mexico or something related to our work. Then I will read the morning paper and
my breviary and go to chapel for thirty or forty minutes.

It is now nearly one o'clock which is time for my next
morphine injection. The injection itself is an experience in pain. I
have no muscle or flesh so getting the needle in and then the
contents into my body is not so simple, but, it seems to help. Then
I am put back on my exercise bike and go through the motions.
After this, I am put in bed and the Sisters give me an hour or two
of physical therapy, range-of-motion movement and ALS massage. During this time, I listen to a tape recording of some book of

the Bible or some spiritual work. Now, I am listening to, "The Last Conversation of St. Therese of Lisieux." This is a marvelous book second only to her autobiography.

I first made the acquaintance of St. Therese at the age of sixteen when I was in the minor seminary. It was my first great love affair. She captivated my heart and she has been a very special friend all my life. I have been annoyed with her because I feel she has forgotten me of late. But in listening to this last conversation she has renewed her friendship and affection and reappeared when I need her most. So she is very much with me once again.

Therese, I thank God for giving you to the Church and to me. You call yourself Little Flower but you are the most beautiful, fragrant, exquisite rose in God's mystical garden. Truly, you are a miracle of God, a beautiful jewel, you are one of His greatest masterpieces. Therese, I love you dearly. I am so grateful for your inspiration and your help in my moment of need.

But at times, forgive me for saying this, I find you very annoying and even infuriating. In your last illness, you endure incredible pain. You speak of your temptation to suicide. You say you never dreamed there could be such pain and you long for a speedy end. You say you can endure no more. When you speak like this, I smile, because, I can relate to you and identify with you at this level.

But then, you go on to say that you would be content to suffer this pain for eternity, if this was pleasing to God. You say you are indifferent to whether you live or die and you endure all with such perfect patience, such model gentleness and such heroism that I am personally ready to despair and give up.

Sometimes, I secretly envy you. No doubt your pain is horrible, but, I compare it to my situation and I say that at least you could move. At least, you could talk. Also, you are surrounded by your own sisters, people of the same culture and you could communicate so easily and draw comfort from their understanding. But, I cannot move my little finger to scratch my ear. I can no longer speak. I have no privacy, whatsoever. Also, the Sisters who care for me are true angels, self-sacrificing, loving, caring, modest and sweet. Yet, they are of different cultures and nationalities and, yes, they are of different genders. Sometimes, it would seem so nice to be surrounded by male companions, preferably priests or brothers of the same nationality, culture and background.

Also, you are of a passive, contemplative disposition. So it is easier for one of this temperament to endure sickness and inactivity. So, I sometimes wonder, if you were me, would you say what you say in your last conversations? The answer, of course, is I have no doubt that you would, because, you are a saint, a hero, one of God's world-class champions. I struggle and huff and puff and try my best, but I simply am not on your level.

It is like comparing two marathon runners. One easily completes the course in two hours, seven minutes and he does it with a minimum of pain. The other, myself, completes the same course in three hours, nineteen minutes and the pain is much greater because by nature, talent and training I am much less prepared. So running in the wake of a champion can be inspiring, but, Therese, at the same time it can be a bit demoralizing and frustrating. Please take no offense at what I say here. I am sure you understand my meaning.

Also, I admire your perfect patience, but, in a sense, I am grateful that I am not such a model of patience and gentleness. I'm afraid if I were, those about me would overwhelm me with praise and admiration. This would be more than I could handle in my present weakened state. Already, I have heard such extravagant remarks and such fulsome praise. If added to this, I could see this remarkable patience and heroic courage in myself, I might be tempted to pride. As it is, I try my best but perfect patience is not a grace which has been given me, or gentleness or sweetness of disposition. So, in a sense, I am grateful for this.

Additionally, Therese, I can identify more with Jesus in the Garden of Gethsemane than with you your sick bed. Jesus is very clear in His inner state. He wants to escape from the passion. He wants to avoid the pain. He does not want this suffering and death and expresses this in His prayer and He shows this in His agony of bloody sweat and His crying of despair on Calvary.

This is my prayer, Lord, take it away. I do not say, let it go on forever. I cannot say it, but, if there is no way out — so be it. I will do my best and ask You to give me the courage. This is the prayer of Jesus. It shows He is human, made of flesh and blood. But

Therese, your prayer is holier than that of Jesus. It seems super-human and it is. At times it is something I admire and I would like to emulate. But, at least at this stage of the game, it is above and beyond me. So, I ask you to change my mind and heart, so they resemble yours and, that, eventually, I can say this prayer and imitate your patience and courage.

Another thing, which I like in your last conversation, are your remarks about the presence of the devil. He is always there in our moments of physical weakness. We see him in the Garden. He is there on Calvary. I am very aware that the devil is in the wings. He is hissing, snapping, snarling and doing his best to rob me of my peace of heart. At times, I am tormented by the wildest fantasies imaginable, but, I won't go into detail. My tactic is simply to call the name of "Mary" and the devil scurries at the sound of this name. Also, the devil is intelligent, so I reason with him. "Fine," I say, "my dear satan, you continue with your torments and temptations. Their only purpose or their net result is to make me experience my weakness and helplessness and sinfulness. So, they leave me more humble and pure and more perfect than before. So, can't you see that God is making a fool of you and using you to defeat your purposes? So, why don't you just give up and with your tail between your legs crawl and hide in a corner somewhere." He usually responds to these remarks and does that very thing.

To get back, after this lengthy digression, to my daily routine, after the afternoon therapy, I have lunch. Usually, I watch a video to distract me from the painful exercise of eating. After this, I try to lay in bed quietly for thirty minutes or so. Then I am put in my wheelchair. I go to chapel to spend an hour or two. Usually, it is a prayer of going in and out of this coma of sleepiness and drowsiness, but, there is great strength and power which emanates from the Eucharist and simply by resting in the presence of this little piece of bread, the strength and power of Christ enters and strengthens me. At five o'clock I am taken to the roof chapel where I listen to the confessions of the children. Then, a little before six I am brought to my room, where, I am given another injection of morphine and put in bed to rest for thirty minutes or so before attacking my evening meal. The problem with me is, not only getting the food inside, but, once inside, absorbing and digesting the nutrition. My GI tract is in a terrible state and I am almost neurotic concerning eating and drinking. I eat very little and the supper goes down more easily by watching television. But, if I make a mistake and eat anything that is difficult to digest, I spend the whole night without sleeping and with great inner discomfort.

After supper, Sister will put me back in the recliner and turn on a tape of the rosary and I follow the prayers of the rosary in my mind. Afterwards, she returns and I watch a little more television. Then, I spend another hour in bed for my evening physical therapy. Again, I listen to a spiritual tape but frequently my mind is so drowsy that I am unaware of what is being said. Following therapy, I am put in my recliner where I watch TV for twenty or thirty minutes. Then, the Sisters leave me alone for fifteen or twenty minutes. I am already dozing, but, I don't want to go to bed too early because the nights are long and it is a real challenge to make it through to the dawn of another day.

I take some more medication before going to sleep. The Sisters have prepared a bed with a special medical mattress, foam-crate sponge, sheepskin and several sheets to make it as comfortable as possible. They place me on my side. Everything has to be just right. Then they sprinkle me with holy water and wish me luck and leave me to the dark and the challenge of the night.

I wake up after an hour or two with my ribs, side or shoulder hurting. I call Sister and she changes my position. I have a limited number of options. Because of the arthritis on my right side, I am restricted to my left side or my back. Also, although the temperature in the room is between 75 and 80 degrees, I find my hands and arms are very cold. Sister massages them, gets them warm, gets me adjusted again and leaves. Some nights are worse than others. Sometimes I get only a few hours of troubled sleep. Other nights I get five or six hours. That's the way it goes.

However, it promises to get much worse. Looking down the road I might have another month or two left. I certainly hope it is no longer. Most likely I will not be able to eat so maybe I will consider a gastrostomy. I don't mind lying in bed trying to rest but because of the pain from the bones and the trembling it is difficult to get comfortable in any posture or position. However, I will do my best and try to take it one day at a time.

Also, in this final chapter I would like to share a few secrets. A priest friend recently asked if I was angry or depressed or frustrated by this ALS sickness. I answered, "no." Somehow I felt I was destined for this all my life. In fact, I had a premonition that something like this was waiting for me down the road. To explain this without sounding mystical or neurotic is not easy. But, I will try.

In my early twenties, I prayed or contemplated in a very romantic, sentimental, idealistic manner of encountering great suffering, sickness or a trial. If, I were to come through this, I would come out purified and perfected. I longed for this and prayed for this. If I realized that ALS was the answer to my prayers, I doubt if I would have continued in this vein. But, somehow, this seems to be exactly what was in my imagination or my prayers over forty years ago. Is this the workings of extra sensory perception or a mystical experience of grace or both? I think it's both. But, at any rate, years ago I thought I was being prepared for this terrible ordeal.

In addition, when I was in high school, I was obsessed with eating. I had great difficulty in controlling my desire for food especially sweets. This caused me a lot of inner torment. Strangely, at the time, there was a clear voice or idea in my inner self which said that at one point in your life you will want to eat but will not be able to do so. So, don't worry about the situation now. You will regret this moment in life, where, you can eat to your heart's content. This kept recurring to me again and again. I laughed and dismissed it and said to myself, "That will be the day, the day I will want to eat and cannot." Well, it is here and I had a preview of coming attractions more than forty years ago.

Also, over the years in my spiritual mansion, I could see the image of myself disabled, unable to use my limbs, and totally at the mercy of others for everything. This total loss of privacy and independence filled me with a sense of terror and panic. I dismissed these ideas from my mind as being unrealistic, but they kept coming back. Here I am and the reality is here. It seems I had many little hints and quiet preparation for where I am right now.

Also, of late I have been thinking of my burial. It matters little to me where my mortal remains end up. I think the Philippines would be the most logical choice and I would prefer Silang because of its beautiful, expansive property. The work in Korea seems to be winding down and the Philippines is our headquarters and our future seems to be based here. So, this would be a logical choice for my tomb.

I would be happy with a hole in the ground and a little plaque saying something like this, "Here lies Al Schwartz. He tried his best for Jesus." That's it. But I think for the good of the Sisters and my children something a little more elaborate would be helpful.

I would like to build a replica of the Shrine of Our Lady of Banneux here on the Silang property. I would like to be buried in the Shrine under the altar at the feet of Our Lady. Mary of Banneux chose me at an early age just as she erupted in the night in the life of Marietta Beco. She suddenly appeared in my life without any preparation. She brought me to Belgium where I discovered her. I never heard of Banneux before then. So my priesthood in a special way belongs to Our Lady of Banneux. My apostolate is hers and I would like to be buried at her feet and say, that, all praise, honor and glory for anything good accomplished in my life goes to her and to her alone.

*   *   *   *   *   *

On March 16, 1992, Father Al Schwartz died in the Philippines.

"All praise, honor, glory and thanksgiving to the Virgin of the Poor!"

Epilogue

A period of mourning followed the death of Father Al Schwartz. A chapel was set up in the gymnasium at the Girlstown in Manila. Then his body was moved to the Boystown in Silang, Cavite, Philippines where Father Al is now buried. Simultaneously, chapels were set up in Talisay, Cebu, Philippines; Pusan and Seoul, Korea; Chalco, Mexico, and for ten days during the wake, the sisters, children, parents, graduates, TB patients, officials, dignataries and various religious groups came to pray and say goodbye. Also, the three superior sisters of the Sisters of Mary in Korea, Sister Sophia Kim, Sister Juliana Heo, Sister Cecilia Shin and over eighty graduates from the Korean program attended. On March 25, 1992, His Eminence Jaime Cardinal Sin officiated at the concelebrated funeral Mass for Father Al with Bishop Jose Maria Hernandez from Mexico and twenty-five priests joining him. Over five thousand people attended the Mass. The saddest moment came when the children sang, "Oh, Mein Papa." Cardinal Sin told the children not to be sad. He said, "Your future is assured because Father Al is now in Heaven and he is near God. Father Al's programs will go on because he can continue to plead for your welfare." Father Al's programs have continued.

June 29, 1992   Dedication of the Virgin of the Poor Chapel, Father Al's Final Resting Place, Silang, Philippines; His Eminence Jaime Cardinal Sin officiated

August 1992	Purchased property in Minglanilla, Cebu, future home for 2,000 boys
October 1992	Construction of a new five-story building in the Village of Homeless Men, Kaengsaengwon, Seoul, Korea
October 1992	Sisters of Mary visit Germany, Switzerland, Belgium and the United States; Sister Michaela Kim, Philippines; Sister Sophia Kim, Korea; and Sister Elena Belarmino, Mexico
November 9, 1992	Inauguration of second building In Chalco (Now serving 1,600 boys and girls) Chalco, Mexico, Bishop Jose Maria Hernandez officiated
March 2, 1993	The Sisters of Mary received official recognition from Rome as a Religious Congregation
March 19, 1993	Inauguration of third building in Talisay, Cebu, Philippines, His Eminence Ricardo Cardinal Vidal officiated